JOURNEY THROUGH

HISTORY

JOURNEY THROUGH

HISTORY

NEIL GRANT

GALLERY BOOKS
An Imprint of W. H. Smith Publishers Inc.
112 Madison Avenue
New York City 10016

First published in the United States in 1991 by Gallery Books,
an imprint of W.H. Smith Publishers, Inc.,
112 Madison Avenue, New York, New York 10016
By arrangement with Reed International Books,
Michelin House, 81 Fulham Road, London SW3 6RB

ISBN 0-8317-5271-8

Printed in Italy

Gallery Books are available for bulk purchase for sales promotions
and premium use. For details write or telephone the Manager of
Special Sales, W.H. Smith Publishers, Inc., 112 Madison Avenue,
New York, New York 10016. (212) 532-6600

CONTENTS

THE ANCIENT WORLD

The First Cities 6
Ancient Egypt 8
Mesopotamia 10
Crete and Mycenae 12
The Greek World 14
The Roman Empire 16
The People of Israel 18

THE MEDIEVAL WORLD

The Franks and Vikings 20
The Norman Age 22
The Christian Church 24
The Byzantine Empire 26
The Rise of Islam 28
Medieval Europe 30
Chinese Civilization 32
Japanese Civilization 34
Indian Civilization 36

REFORM AND REVOLUTION

Renaissance Europe 38
The New World 40
The Reformation 42

Muslim Emperors 44
Wars of Religion 46
An Age of Absolutism 48
American Independence 50
The French Revolution 52

THE MODERN WORLD

Machines and Factories 54
The Railroad Age 56
The American Civil War 58
African Civilizations 60
The Power of the West 62
Peace and Prosperity 64
The German Empire 66
World War I 68
The New Dictators 70
World War II 72
The Post-War World 74
New Ways of Living 76

Index 78

Acknowledgments 80

Time Chart

THE FIRST CITIES

A journey through history does not have a beginning. We cannot say exactly when human beings appeared on earth, although the first people like us probably lived about 40,000 years ago. These humans of the early Stone Age sheltered in caves or rough "houses" made of branches and fashioned tools from stone and other natural materials such as bone and wood. They depended directly on nature for everything they needed, and spent most of their time getting food by hunting wild animals and gathering wild plants. They did not stay in one place for long, but moved to wherever food could be found, often following herds of reindeer and oxen as they migrated.

The people of the Stone Age lived in the same way for thousands of years. Change, which happens so quickly today, was almost unknown then.

The Food Growers

Change did happen, however, although very slowly. The first great change in history was the change from a life of hunting and gathering to a life of farming.

People began to grow a kind of wheat in the Middle East over 10,000 years ago. Villagers in Southeast Asia began to grow millet. In Mexico and Central America, too, farming developed independently, although much later. There, the chief crop was corn.

As well as growing crops, people also began to tame and raise animals. Wild sheep and goats roamed the grasslands of the Middle East, and gradually people began to take over some of these herds. Pigs, cattle, and horses came later.

The introduction of farming brought many other major changes with it. Most importantly, it allowed people to settle in one place – a family which lives by hunting and gathering needs thousands of acres to provide enough food, but a family which lives by farming needs only ten to 20 acres. This new, more stable life meant the population began to grow.

Farming also produced more food, often more than was needed. As a result, successful farmers could trade their extra food for goods produced by neighboring people. In addition, farming took up less time. It was no longer necessary for everyone to spend most of the day hunting for food. Society became divided into different classes of people, with some working in the fields and others doing different jobs.

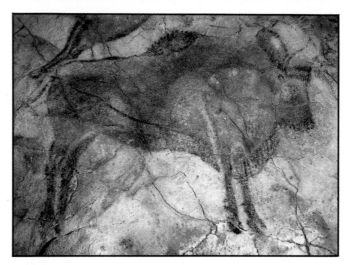

Above: Jericho is one of the oldest cities in the world. Archaeologists have discovered there the remains of walls and a tower which were built in the New Stone Age, nearly 12,000 years ago.

FIRST CROPS AND FARM ANIMALS INTRODUCED IN THE MIDDLE EAST c.9000 B.C.

Left: Ancient paintings of animals were found on the walls of buried caves in southern France and northern Spain about 100 years ago. Some of them are over 20,000 years old. They show that the human beings of the Old Stone Age were skilful artists – many thousands of years before "civilization" began.

Town Life

Because people had more time and work was more varied, new discoveries were made and changes happened more quickly than they had in the past. By about 6000 B.C., plates and pots were being molded out of clay and baked in ovens. Before 3000 B.C., potters in the Middle East began to make pots and vessels on a wheel. This may have been the first use for wheels, but they were soon being fitted to carts, which were pulled by oxen. Animals also pulled the plow, which was invented about the same time. The first plows were very simple. The part that cultivated the soil was no more than a heavy stick with a point which had been hardened in a fire. Nevertheless, these simple machines made farming quicker and easier.

After farming, the most important discovery of prehistoric times was the use of metal to make tools and weapons. The earliest metal objects were made of copper and bronze. Iron is a better metal for tools, but it is harder to make, so was not used until about 1,500 years later. By that time, town life was well established in some parts of the world. The earliest settled farming villages, dating from about 5000 B.C., did not produce a written language or large stone buildings or other features of what we call "civilization." They did, however, create places where civilization could develop, although this did not happen until about 2,000 years later.

Right: Pottery was one of the earliest crafts. The first pots were modeled with the hands as early as 10,000 B.C.

Left: The invention of the potter's wheel made a huge difference. Modern potters use the same methods as this man.

BRONZE FIRST MADE c.4000 B.C. • PLOW AND WHEEL INVENTED c.3500 B.C.

ANCIENT EGYPT

The first civilizations grew up in river valleys. In Egypt, the Nile provided water, and its yearly flood covered the valley with a layer of mud so rich that farmers could grow two or three crops a year. On each side of the valley lay the desert, which guarded Egypt from attack. Protected by the desert and the sea and nourished by the Nile, the civilization of ancient Egypt lasted longer than any other civilization, even that of China.

For most of its 3,000 year span, during the periods of the Old, Middle, and New Kingdoms (see dates below right), ancient Egyptian civilization flourished. Life, however, was not always peaceful, and for long periods government broke down completely. Despite this, civilization survived. When Egypt was finally conquered by Alexander the Great in 332 B.C., life was still in many ways the same as it had been when King Menes united the cities of Upper and Lower Egypt as one kingdom in about 3100 B.C.

Gods and People

The ruler of Egypt was called a pharaoh. He was not only a king, but was also considered to be a god. He was worshipped along with many other gods, such as Ra, the Sun god, Horus, the falcon-headed god, and Thoth, the ibis-headed god of wisdom.

Below the pharaoh came nobles and priests, then the scribes or clerks who kept a record of government business, and finally farmers, craftsmen, and slave-workers, who were usually prisoners of war.

Most people worked on the land, growing wheat, barley, vegetables, grapes for wine, and flax for linen. They kept sheep, goats, pigs, and cattle, and rich men hunted wildfowl, even hippos, in the Nile Delta. The Egyptians also traded with other people around the Mediterranean, and sent ships down the Red Sea to East Africa for special goods such as frankincense.

Taxes were high, and besides having to give part of their crop in payment, ordinary people had to work on building the temples, pyramids, and tombs of the pharaohs. When the pyramids were built, the Egyptians did not have wheels or levers. They used rollers to move the stone blocks along ramps. Because they did not have any iron, they cut the stone with copper chisels. The buildings were enormous. The Great Pyramid of King Khufu at Giza was about 500 ft high.

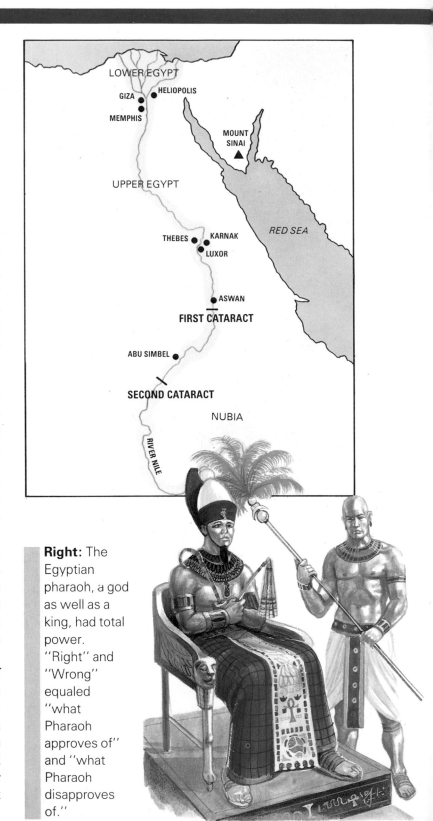

Right: The Egyptian pharaoh, a god as well as a king, had total power. "Right" and "Wrong" equaled "what Pharaoh approves of" and "what Pharaoh disapproves of."

UPPER AND LOWER EGYPT UNITED AS ONE KINGDOM BY KING MENES IN c.3100 B.C.

Left: Ancient Egypt was a
strangely shaped land,
like a flower with a stem.
The Egyptian climate is
too dry for crops. Only the
Nile River made farming
possible – by flooding
every year and covering
its valley with rich mud.

Left: The finest pyramids
still standing are at Giza
on the outskirts of
modern Cairo. They are
guarded by the Sphinx, a
sculpture of a lion with a
human head, which was
carved out of a huge rock.

Tombs and Mummies

The Egyptians believed that a human soul lived on
after death, but it needed a body, too. For this reason
they preserved the bodies of important people by
mummification – taking out the insides, soaking the
bodies in a kind of soda, then drying and
wrapping them with bandages. Buried inside
several coffins deep in a stone tomb, a body
could be preserved for centuries.

The tombs contained treasures,
as well as useful items for the
next life. One contained a model
brewery so the dead pharaoh
could drink beer! The walls were
painted with scenes from the
dead person's life, showing his
family, servants, and possessions.
These paintings, and sculptures
found in the tombs, tell us most
of what we know about life in
ancient Egypt.

Below: This gold pendant
is in the form of a vulture,
the sacred bird of Mut, an
Egyptian goddess.

OLD KINGDOM 2700–2150 B.C. • MIDDLE KINGDOM 2040–1670 B.C. • NEW KINGDOM 1570–1080 B.C.

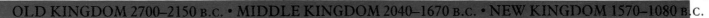

MESOPOTAMIA

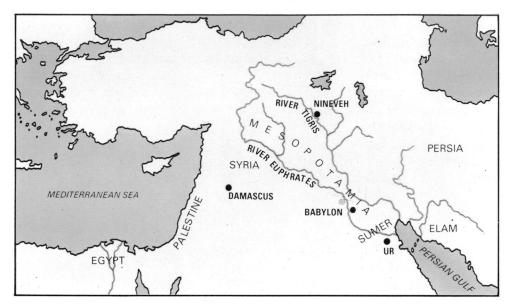

Mesopotamia means "the land between two rivers," that is between the Tigris and Euphrates rivers in what is roughly modern Iraq. In the south, the land was flat, swampy, and hot. The Sumerians, who settled there before 4000 B.C., had to build dikes and canals to keep fields watered and settlements dry.

Sumerian Cities

The Sumerians had a complicated and powerful religion, and their cities grew up around religious shrines which were the homes of local gods. At Ur, the most famous of the Sumerian cities, the home of the god who "owned" the city was on top of a high ziggurat (a pyramid built in steps). Because each city had its own gods and its own ruler, the Sumerians were not a united people and often fought one another.

Sumerian cities were built of brick made from river mud which was baked hard. Even the largest temples and palaces were often built of mud bricks because the Sumerians had neither building stone nor wood, except what they gained through trade.

Rich citizens in Sumer seem to have lived well. In their tombs, archaeologists have found beautiful jewelry and fine clothes, as well as board games and musical instruments.

Sumerian civilization lasted about 1,500 years. Although Sumer suffered wars and conquest, the invaders copied many Sumerian customs. Perhaps the most important of these was cuneiform (wedge-shaped)

writing, which was cut into clay tablets using "pens" made of reeds. By about 2000 B.C., Sumerian civilization had spread to many parts of the Middle East. Not long after then, the Sumerians died out as a separate people, but Sumerian civilization lived on, in changing forms, among the new races and nations which rose to power in Mesopotamia.

SUMERIAN CIVILIZATION c.3500–2000 B.C. • BABYLONIAN EMPIRE (OLD AND NEW) 2100–539 B.C.

Middle Eastern Empires

Settled villages and rich cities attracted attacks from people whose life was not settled, and the history of early civilizations in the Middle East is a story of invasions and conquests, of the rise and fall of empires. The greatest empires were those of the Assyrians and Babylonians, whose capital was a city of luxurious gardens and works of art. Other states rose and fell, each giving something to the advance of human knowledge, even if it was only some original idea in the art of warfare.

The Assyrians were the most successful warriors. They came to control an empire stretching from Egypt to the Persian Gulf. In the seventh century B.C., however, their empire grew too large to control and collapsed when attacked by the New Babylonians.

In about the middle of the sixth century B.C., a formidable new power arose, that of the Persians led by Cyrus the Great. Cyrus conquered an empire larger than any which had existed before, stretching from the Nile River to the Indus River.

Right and below: This jar, rhinoceros seal (for making an impression in damp clay), and board game, were all found in the Indus River valley.

The Indus River Valley

The earliest center of civilization in India was the Indus River valley (now in Pakistan). It covered a large area, for its two greatest cities, Mohenjo-daro and Harappa, were about 1,000 miles apart. These cities had streets arranged in a grid pattern, the earliest example of town planning. They also had good drains and sewers and buildings of brick. The Indus River valley was more fertile in prehistoric times than it is today, and farmers grew wheat, barley, mustard, dates, melons, cotton, and probably rice. They kept cattle and water buffalo, and may have used elephants to carry trade goods. They also had dogs and cats.

The statues, jewelry, and models or toys from this period which have been found by archaeologists are in a style recognized as typically Indian. Yet, the Indus River valley people disappeared after invaders from the northwest overran the country in approximately 1500 B.C.

Left: This helmet was discovered in the Sumerian city of Ur. It is made from a sheet of gold, and has holes for laces to hold a pad on the inside, making it comfortable to wear.

ASSYRIAN EMPIRE c.1100–612 B.C. • INDUS RIVER VALLEY CIVILIZATION c.2600–1500 B.C.

CRETE AND MYCENAE

Before 2000 B.C., a remarkable civilization developed in the fertile island of Crete in the eastern Mediterranean. This civilization was only discovered early this century, by the British archaeologist Sir Arthur Evans, and is called Minoan, after Minos, the legendary Cretan king.

King Minos's capital was Knossos, which at that time was the greatest city ever built, perhaps holding more than 100,000 people. The royal palace was five stories high and covered twice as much ground as a football field. It contained not only apartments for the ruler, but also accommodation and workshops for many other members of the community.

The wealth of Minoan Crete depended on the sea. Fishing provided both work and food for many, while some sailed merchant ships to Egypt, Greece, and other regions to exchange goods such as textiles and pottery. The sea also protected the Minoans from invasions. Minoan Crete must have been peaceful, as they did not build defensive walls around their towns.

The Minoans developed several forms of writing. One of them we still do not understand, but the other was an early form of Greek. The Minoans may also have influenced the religion of classical Greece, although the chief Minoan deity was a goddess, not a god.

Below: In the palaces of Minoan Crete a strange ritual took place, in which athletic young people vaulted over bulls. It was probably a kind of religious ceremony rather than a sport.

Mycenae

Minoan civilization disappeared in 1500–1400 B.C., and the people who took over in Crete were the Mycenaeans, the dominant race on the Greek mainland. They had little culture of their own when they first arrived in Greece, and the civilization which did evolve owed a great deal to Minoan Crete.

Their political system was, however, their own. Each of their cities was independent and had its own king, although they sometimes acted together. When they did so, it was often under the leadership of the king of Mycenae, the greatest city on the mainland. Beneath each king was a class of landowning warriors,

MINOAN CIVILIZATION c.2500–1400 B.C. • MYCENAEAN CIVILIZATION c.1600–1200 B.C.

who controlled the mass of peasants and slaves.

The Mycenaeans took over the trade and colonies of the Minoans and became equally wealthy. One of their trading posts was at Troy, and the siege of Troy, the story told by the Greek poet Homer in the *Iliad*, is probably based on real events which took place around 1200 B.C. By that time, however, things were changing in the Mediterranean world. A new race, the Dorians, was invading Greece from the north, and Mycenaean civilization gradually disappeared.

The Phoenicians

The people known as the Phoenicians settled on what is now the coast of Lebanon before 2000 B.C. They never created a single state (although at various times one of their cities dominated the others), and were usually under the rule of more powerful nations. In about the twelfth century B.C., following the collapse of Mycenaean power, however, the Phoenicians seized their opportunity.

Phoenician power was based on the sea. The Phoenicians were the greatest sailors of the ancient world, and ventured as far as West Africa and even Cornwall in England, where they traded for tin. They were successful in trade largely because of the rare goods they had to exchange. Although their territory was small, it contained timber, which was in short supply in the rest of the Middle East. They also traded carved ivory, and an expensive purple dye, which was made from a kind of shellfish. They may have been the first people to make vessels by blowing glass.

The Phoenicians were responsible for one huge advance in civilization – the alphabet. They noticed that the number of sounds used in language is actually quite small, so they invented a symbol (or, we should say, a letter) for each sound. These symbols are the basis of the alphabet we still use today.

The Phoenician homeland was overrun by the Assyrians in the seventh century B.C., but their colonies survived, notably Carthage in North Africa. This grew to be a great power in its own right, with city walls about 70 miles long and a huge harbor protected by chains. In the fourth century B.C., however, a new power arose in the Mediterranean – Rome. The rivalry between Carthage and Rome ended eventually in the destruction of Carthage in 146 B.C.

Above: Phoenician merchants traveled all over the Mediterranean in their small, sturdy, sailing ships.

Below: The Phoenician alphabet only had 22 letters (all consonants). This is an example of Phoenician script.

FIRST PHOENICIAN CITIES c.2000 B.C. • FOUNDATION OF CARTHAGE c.750 B.C.

13

THE GREEK WORLD

The society of classical Greece marks the beginning of European civilization and history. Following the collapse of the Mycenaean world, Greece entered a Dark Age, but in about 800 B.C. more prosperous times returned, and we can recognize the faint beginnings of what we call classical civilization.

Perhaps the most important characteristic of the Greeks was their ability to change: they made huge advances in human knowledge in just a few centuries. Because the Greeks were a literary people, who produced historians, poets, and novelists, we know a great deal about them. For the first time in history, individual people appear to us as real human beings, whom we can understand.

The City-State

The typical Greek community was a city and its surrounding area. The Greeks did not form a nation with a central government until the days of Alexander the Great (see below).

The city-state was something much more than a local council or a government. It was a real community, almost like a very large family. In Athens, every citizen was expected to take part in the assembly, where laws were made and policies decided, and to vote for the officials who ran the government. Not everyone, however, was a citizen. Women did not have the right to vote and neither did slaves.

Literature, Art, and Science

It is very unlikely that the human race will ever produce people who are more intelligent than the ancient Greeks. The difference between the Greeks and us is that we know more, not that we are more clever. Aristotle was the chief authority in the study of biology, physics, psychology, and many other subjects for

DARK AGE OF GREECE c.1200–800 B.C. • ARCHAIC PERIOD 800–500 B.C.

about 2,000 years. No real advance was made on Greek knowledge of geometry and arithmetic until the seventeenth century. The only drawback to Greek science was that, while it produced many brilliant ideas, these were not always tested by experiment, which modern scientists say is essential. As a result, the Greeks got some facts wrong.

The Greeks practiced nearly every form of literature, and invented many. They were the first to produce plays that were not simply religious in purpose. The Greek idea of dramatic tragedy, seen at its best in the works of Aeschylus, Sophocles, and Euripides, is still powerful today.

Greek art and architecture have had an equally powerful influence. Some of the Greeks' finest buildings, like the Parthenon, in Athens, are still standing, and many museums have examples of classical Greek sculpture. In their search for perfection, Greek sculptors made the most realistic – and beautiful – human figures of any age.

Greek religion involved the worship of a great number of different gods and goddesses, including Zeus, the king of the gods. These deities were in many ways like ordinary people, but with superhuman powers. They had human form – and human problems. This is a sign of the Greeks' deep interest in humankind. For the gods to behave like people was natural. The fact that a god might lose his temper or misbehave did not mean that he was not respected.

Alexander the Great

In 338 B.C., Greece was conquered by King Philip of Macedon, a state to the north. Greek independence came to an end, but Greek civilization expanded, for the Macedonians soon became "Greeks" themselves.

Alexander, Philip's son, was an extraordinary man, whose ambition was to create a single civilization. In 334 B.C. he attacked the huge empire of Persia, an old enemy of the Greeks, and rapidly conquered it. He went on with his great military campaigns until his personal empire covered most of the known world, as far as the Punjab in India. Alexander died, aged only 32, in 323 B.C., and his empire broke up into separate sections. By that time, however, Greek civilization had been spread over the whole Mediterranean region, and even into the lands of the older civilizations of the Middle East.

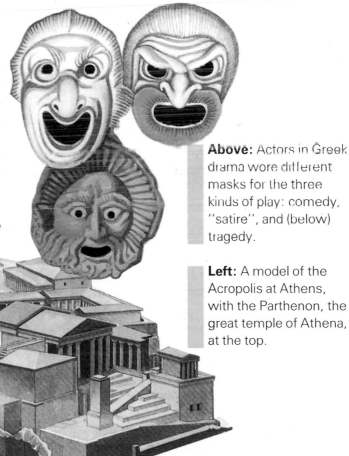

Above: Actors in Greek drama wore different masks for the three kinds of play: comedy, "satire", and (below) tragedy.

Left: A model of the Acropolis at Athens, with the Parthenon, the great temple of Athena, at the top.

CLASSICAL PERIOD 500–330 B.C. • HELLENISTIC AGE 330–100 B.C.

15

THE ROMAN EMPIRE

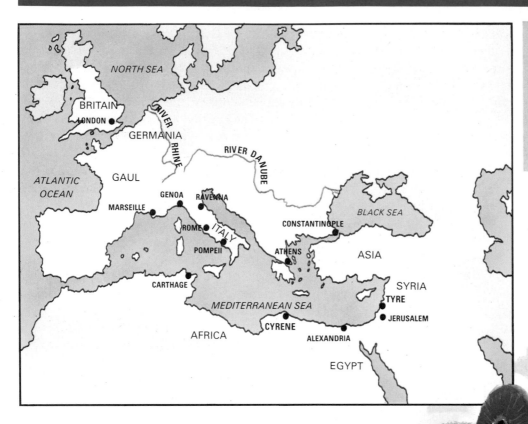

In about 600 years, Rome grew from a few villages on the River Tiber in Italy to a great empire which stretched from Britain to the Persian Gulf. It covered over 2 million square miles and included over 50 million people. Roman civilization influenced the whole world, and it continued to do so for centuries after the empire itself had disappeared.

The empire was gained – and defended – by the highly trained Roman army of full-time professional soldiers. Roman military power enabled the people of the empire to live in peace, governed by the excellent laws which the Romans established. Everywhere, educated people spoke Latin, the Roman language, and followed Roman customs. As a rule, however, the Romans did not interfere too much with local traditions. For example, all kinds of religions were allowed, although people were expected to respect the gods of Rome as well. People who belonged to the new religion of Christianity were sometimes persecuted because they refused to worship the Roman emperor as a god. Yet, eventually, Christianity became the official faith of the empire.

Above: When attacking a fort, Roman soldiers formed a "tortoise" with their shields as a defence against missiles.

TRADITIONAL DATE OF FOUNDING OF ROME 753 B.C. • ROMAN REPUBLIC 509–27 B.C.

16

Roman Civilization

The Romans were skilled builders and engineers. They built aqueducts, bridges, roads, temples, palaces, and public buildings. The drains and water supply in a Roman town were better than any that were built in Europe until the nineteenth century.

The rulers of Rome often organized extravagant entertainments. Some of these – Christians being thrown to wild animals, fights to the death between gladiators – showed the worst side of Roman civilization. The Romans, however, also produced fine poets, like Horace, Ovid and Virgil and historians like Livy and Tacitus.

Republic and Empire

For centuries Rome was a republic, in which all citizens had some share in government. A growing struggle between the nobles and the masses, however, ended in a century of civil war and dictatorship.

In 49 B.C., Julius Caesar, one of Rome's greatest generals, seized power. He was soon murdered because other nobles feared he would make himself emperor. Yet, his adopted son and successor, Octavian, did become emperor, taking the name Augustus in 27 B.C. He was a wise and capable ruler, but his successors were not, and after the cruel and unstable Nero had been thrown out in A.D. 68, the title of emperor became simply the prize for the most popular general. In fact, this produced some of Rome's best emperors, and under Hadrian, who ruled from A.D. 117–138, Roman civilization reached its height.

East and West

In A.D. 395, the empire was divided in two. The Eastern Empire, with its capital at Byzantium (Constantinople), lasted 1,000 years, but in the West the decline continued, and tribal peoples invaded. The last Roman emperor in the West, Romulus Augustus, was deposed in A.D. 476.

Above: The ruins of the Colosseum in Rome. This great amphitheater could hold 50,000 people, who came to watch bloodthirsty sports.

Right: Julius Caesar, whose fame as a conqueror and skill as a politician made him the ruler of Rome in 49 B.C.

THE PEOPLE OF ISRAEL

The ancient Hebrews, or Israelites, were not very numerous and for nearly all of their history were ruled by others. Their religion, Judaism, however, was a powerful force in shaping civilization. Two of the greatest world religions, Christianity and Islam, owe much to it.

Judaism, with its belief in a single, all-powerful god – all previous religions had many gods – developed around 1200 B.C., at the time when Moses was leading the Israelites out of Egypt to the Promised Land

Right: The Temple of Solomon, built in the tenth century B.C., probably looked something like this. It was not meant to hold worshippers, but was a more permanent version of the Tabernacle, the holy shrine which the Israelites carried with them.

of Canaan (Palestine).

Although the Hebrews had to fight other settlers, such as the Philistines (descendants of Phoenician colonists), by 1000 B.C. they had formed a united kingdom under King David, who made his capital at Jerusalem. Later, the kingdom split into two, with Israel in the north and Judea in the south. Israel disappeared in 721 B.C. when the region was overrun and conquered by the Assyrians.

In the sixth century B.C., the Babylonians took over Judea, and carried off most of the Jews to exile in Babylon. When the Persians conquered Babylon in 539 B.C., they allowed the exiles to return, and at first the religion of the Jews, as these survivors were called, was tolerated by their new rulers. In 167 B.C., however, the ruler of the time tried to impose Greek customs, and in defense of their religion and way of life, the Jews started a rebellion and won their independence under Judas Maccabeus.

The Jews' new-found freedom lasted for about 100 years, until Roman rule was imposed in 63 B.C. Jesus of Nazareth was born and died under Roman rule, but about 30 years after the Crucifixion, the Jews rebelled again. This time, the Romans crushed them. In A.D. 70, Jerusalem was destroyed, and many Jews joined the Diaspora (Dispersion), the name given to Jews living in other countries. The Jewish state disappeared and was not created again until 1948.

HEBREWS LED TO CANAAN BY MOSES c.1200 B.C. • DAVID BECOMES KING c.1000 B.C.

Judaism and the Bible

The story of the ancient Hebrews is vividly told in the Bible (the Old Testament in the Christian Bible). The books which make up the Bible were written in Hebrew at different times between about 1000 B.C. and 150 B.C.

The Bible explains how, after the Jews' escape from Egypt, they made a covenant, or contract, with God. They promised to worship Him alone, and to obey the Ten Commandments, a set of moral laws which, according to the Bible, were given by God to Moses on Mount Sinai. In return for this, God recognized the Jews as His "Chosen People," and gave them His special protection.

The Jews believed in a Messiah, the "Christ" or Savior, who would lead them to freedom from hated foreign domination. Under Roman rule, several men claimed to be this Messiah. One of them was Jesus of Nazareth. A small group of disciples believed his claim, but the religious leaders of the Jews did not. Jesus was finally executed by crucifixion in about A.D. 29, but his teaching, and the work of disciples like St. Paul, resulted in the new religion of Christianity.

The ideas which were preached and practiced by Jesus had a special appeal for poor people, and Christianity, with its single, all-powerful and all-forgiving God, and its promise of life after death, was a much stronger faith than the old religion of the Roman Empire with its many gods. In spite of hatred, persecution, and competition from other religions, Christianity spread steadily. By the end of the third century A.D., Christianity was widely accepted throughout the Roman Empire. It gradually became organized, and Christian leaders set about collecting the writings that recorded the life and teaching of Jesus – a collection we know as the New Testament.

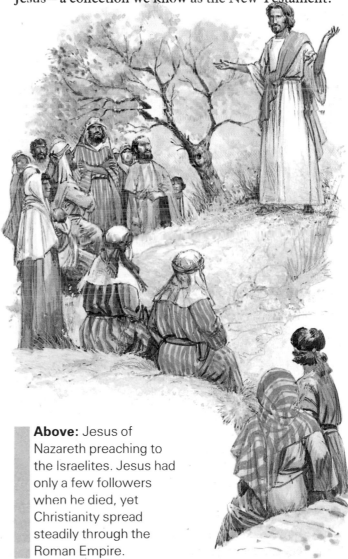

Above: Jesus of Nazareth preaching to the Israelites. Jesus had only a few followers when he died, yet Christianity spread steadily through the Roman Empire.

THE FRANKS AND VIKINGS

Many barbarian kingdoms were set up in the ruins of the Roman Empire, but most soon disappeared. An exception was the kingdom of the Franks. In the fifth century A.D., the Franks were united under Clovis, a Christian who had the support of the Roman church against other Germanic tribes. Clovis's kingdom, however, was not a state like the Roman Empire. It was more like a group of family estates, and after Clovis's death in 511, it was divided up among his sons.

Charlemagne

The Frankish lands were reunited under Charlemagne (a name which means Charles the Great) in the eighth century. He was the grandson of Charles Martel, the great Frankish leader who had stopped the advance of the Muslims into Europe in 732.

Charlemagne created an empire bigger than any since Roman times. He thought of himself as the heir of the Roman Emperors, and in 800 the Pope crowned him Emperor of the Romans. He fought many wars, against the Lombards, Saxons, Byzantines, Serbs, Bretons, Danes, and especially the Muslims.

Charlemagne encouraged scholarship, especially the production of documents (all, of course, handwritten). His court at Aachen became the chief center of European learning and able men came there from all over Europe. Frankish civilization was influenced by ancient Rome, but also by Byzantium and the civilization of Islam. Compared with Muslim Baghdad, or with Constantinople, however, Charlemagne's

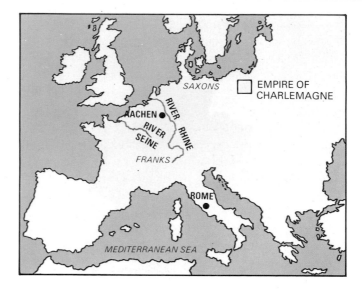

Above: Charlemagne ruled the largest European empire since the fall of Rome. He saw himself as a new "Roman" emperor.

Right: A bronze figure of Thor, the Scandinavian Thunder god. The name Thursday ("Thor's day") comes from him.

empire was rather poor and backward.

The Frankish empire split up soon after Charlemagne's death. The two main divisions were the lands of the West and East Franks, roughly equivalent to modern France and Germany.

Left: Charlemagne's throne in his palace at Aachen (Aix-la-Chapelle) in Germany.

REIGN OF CHARLEMAGNE 768–814 • TREATY OF VERDUN (FRANKISH EMPIRE DIVIDED) 843

Above: The Vikings were good craftsmen as well as good fighters. This hoard of silver, found in England in 1840, shows that some of them were also very rich.

The Vikings

By Charlemagne's time, Europeans lived in settled communities, and most people were Christian. The Scandinavians, however, were not and, with a growing population, they were short of land. This was probably the main reason for the raids of the Vikings, which began in the late eighth century.

Although the Vikings are remembered as raiders and robbers, they were essentially colonists and traders. They raided places as far away as Constantinople, but settled in eastern England, Normandy, and other parts of Europe, as well as in lands where few people lived. Iceland was their most important colony, but the Vikings also founded settlements in Greenland, and they had at least one community in Newfoundland.

The Vikings' voyages would have been impossible without their excellent longships, fast, dragon-like craft, which depended on oars as well as sails. For peaceful voyages, the Vikings had bigger, slower ships.

Once the Vikings had a foothold in a country, colonists usually settled down quite quickly and accepted Christianity. In Iceland, they created a republic, with an assembly of elders and *no* all-powerful king.

Scandinavian Civilization

Iceland was especially important for Scandinavian civilization because it was there that the famous sagas (stories) were written. These sagas, some of them legends and some historical, were one of the glories of European civilization in the early Middle Ages.

The Vikings also had fine artists and craftsmen. Bronze weapons were beautifully made and gilded or silver-plated with powerful, swirling designs.

The vigor and confidence of the Vikings was passed down to their descendants. These included the Normans of Normandy (northwest France) who, in the eleventh century, were to become the greatest European power.

Left: The reason the Scandinavians began raiding their neighbors was not that they were especially warlike or greedy; probably, they were running out of good farm land in their own countries.

FIRST VIKING SETTLEMENT IN ICELAND 874 • NORMANDY GRANTED TO VIKINGS 911

THE NORMAN AGE

By the eleventh century, some kingdoms existed in Europe, but what counted was who held the most land and commanded the most men. Sometimes the heads of great families were stronger than the kings themselves. The most successful rulers, in an age when success was judged by conquest, were the dukes of Normandy. Before the end of the century, the Normans had conquered a kingdom for themselves in southern Italy, which was then under Byzantine rule, and, following the Battle of Hastings in 1066, a Norman duke had taken the Crown of England. These conquests spread Norman ideas and customs through much of Europe and the Mediterranean region.

Feudalism

The way in which society was organized in the Norman lands and throughout most of western Europe between the eleventh and fourteenth centuries is called feudalism, which comes from a Latin word meaning a piece of land. In theory, all land belonged to the king, but he leased most of it to great lords. In return, they swore to be loyal to him and to give him certain services, of which the most important was support in war. Great lords might lease some of their estates to lesser lords, who swore loyalty to them in the same way.

A feudal estate was called a lordship, or, in parts of England, a "manor." It was often roughly the same as a village, with surrounding farm land. Local government, including law enforcement and services like a mill to grind corn, was provided by the lord or his

Below: In a medieval manor house, the main room was often on the upper floor, reached by steps from outside.

NORMAN CONQUEST OF SOUTH ITALY 1030–1091 • NORMAN CONQUEST OF ENGLAND 1066

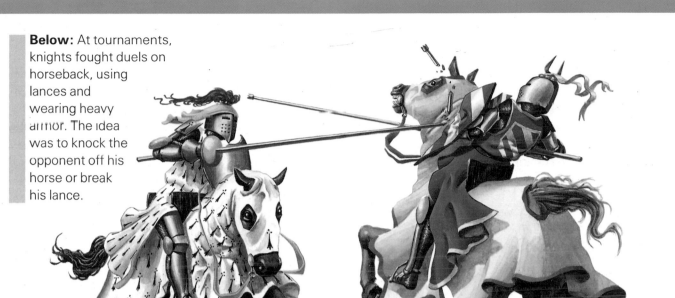

Below: At tournaments, knights fought duels on horseback, using lances and wearing heavy armor. The idea was to knock the opponent off his horse or break his lance.

steward. Some of the land was kept by the lord as his home farm. Some might be rented out to freeholders for money. In general, however, most of the land was worked by serfs.

Although a serf was not a slave, he was not a free man either. He could not leave the manor, nor, for example, marry off his children without the lord's permission. For most of the week, the serf worked his own land, giving part of his produce to the lord, while for one or two days of each week he worked on the lord's home farm.

Every manor had to look after its own needs and very little was bought from outside. Therefore not everyone worked on the land – craftsmen like blacksmiths, carpenters, and millers were also necessary. Ordinary people did not have last names then, and therefore were often described by their craft. That is why last names like Smith and Miller are common in England today.

Some of the land was "common" land, which was rough land, where everyone could let animals graze, or gather firewood. Huge areas of land, however, were

reserved for hunting by the king and his great lords (mainly for deer and wild boar). People caught poaching in this forest land ("forest" did not necessarily mean land covered by trees), were severely punished, sometimes by death.

Life was hard and risky for everyone, but especially for serfs. A poor harvest meant that many people were likely to die of starvation in winter. Few animals could be kept all winter, because there was not enough feed, so most were slaughtered in the autumn, and the meat salted to stop it from going bad. Poor people did not eat meat often, even in good times. They frequently had to manage with soup made from nettles, or bread made from ground acorns.

In many ways, living standards had not changed much in centuries. There were some important improvements, however. Stone buildings were becoming common, although not for the houses of ordinary people. Sheep were kept more widely, and people wore woolen clothes, instead of the skins and furs worn by their ancestors.

UNIVERSITY OF PARIS FOUNDED 1150 • UNIVERSITY OF OXFORD FOUNDED 1167

THE CHRISTIAN CHURCH

In many ways, the most powerful institution in Europe in about 1200 was the church, which owned huge estates in every country. It had almost complete control of education and learning, and of what we should call the news media, for in a world without television or newspapers, people knew little except what they heard from the priest in the pulpit. The church was well organized, and priests were to be found at every level of society, from royal courts to country villages. It even had its own system of law and special courts to enforce it.

Monasteries

The monasteries, especially those belonging to the order founded by an Italian saint called Benedict (480–543), were islands of Christian civilization in the countryside. As well as spending much of their time praying, monks worked the land and cared for the sick and travelers. They also studied and taught, and so were able to spread a knowledge of Christianity throughout the countryside and beyond. Religious communities for women, called convents or nunneries, did similar work.

The Papacy

As head of the church, the Pope had great power and even greater influence. The papacy, however, was not a great military power, and it therefore needed an ally who was. It had found this in the kings of the Carolingian dynasty, and Charlemagne's coronation by the Pope in 800 was the high point of the alliance. Later, the church found a similar ally in the German kings, including Otto the Great in the tenth century, who revived Charlemagne's office of Holy Roman Emperor.

As the religious head of "Christendom," the Pope held authority over not only all clergy, but all *people* – including kings and emperors. At least, that was the Pope's view. Kings and emperors saw things differently. They considered themselves supreme in their own lands. As a result, a conflict of authority arose between church (the Pope) and state (the ruler). The greatest quarrel concerned the right to appoint bishops. Bishops were powerful local figures, just like secular (non-religious) lords, and the rulers wanted their own men in these posts. The Pope, however, wanted men who would put their loyalty to the papacy before their loyalty to any king.

Left: Medieval monasteries were little communities which, like the villages, contained everything needed for everyday life. They grew their own wheat, ground it in their own mill, and baked it in their own bakery. The main difference was that the landowner was the church and the head of the community was the abbot. The job of the monks was, of course, to worship God, but they were also skillful craftsmen, farmers and, sometimes, teachers.

The quarrel came to a head when Pope Gregory VII clashed with Emperor Henry IV. The emperor declared that Gregory was not rightfully pope, and Gregory replied by proclaiming Henry no longer Holy Roman Emperor. This gave some of Henry's subjects an excuse for rebellion. To save his crown, Henry traveled to Canossa in 1077, where he begged forgiveness. Gregory did not want to forgive him, as this meant betraying the rebels, but he had no choice.

By the reign of Pope Innocent III, the papacy was at the height of its power. Signs of its future decline, however, could already be seen. One problem was that it was becoming too political. People felt that the Popes were forgetting their true task, to uphold the Christian religion. Some small groups even broke away from the church altogether. It became the job of the Inquisition, an organization controlled by the Pope, to eliminate such heretics.

Between 1305 and 1377, the papacy was fatally weakened when the Popes left Rome and settled in Avignon, France. From there it was hard for any Pope to claim to be the supreme authority in Christendom. He looked more like a puppet of the king of France. To make matters worse still, for some years after their return to Rome there were two rival Popes, and for a short time even three!

THOMAS BECKET

In England, King Henry II quarreled with Thomas Becket, Archbishop of Canterbury, over the independence of the clergy. In particular, he wanted clergy who were charged with serious crimes to be tried in the ordinary courts, not the church courts. Becket was murdered by a group of knights, who thought, wrongly, that Henry would approve of their action. Becket's death as a martyr forced the king to give up his dispute with the church, and in 1173 Becket was made a saint. His shrine at Canterbury became an important center of pilgrimage.

THE BYZANTINE EMPIRE

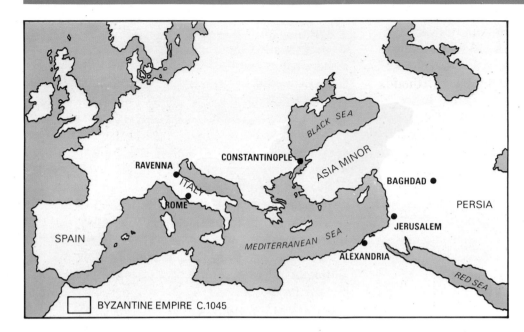

BLACK SEA

CONSTANTINOPLE
ASIA MINOR

RAVENNA

ITALY

ROME

BAGHDAD

PERSIA

SPAIN

JERUSALEM

MEDITERRANEAN SEA

ALEXANDRIA

RED SEA

☐ BYZANTINE EMPIRE C.1045

Left: The Byzantine empire reached its greatest extent under Justinian I (527–565), when it expanded into the lands of ancient Rome. By the middle of the eleventh century it was still quite large, but afterward shrank rapidly under pressure from the Muslims.

While ancient Rome declined, Constantinople grew, until its size and wealth astounded Western visitors. The Byzantines saw themselves not only as continuing the Roman Empire, but as the guardians of Christianity, since the papacy in Rome was not yet powerful. In the sixth century, under the Emperor Justinian, who is remembered for his reform of the system of Roman law, the Byzantine empire stretched around the Mediterranean, including much of Italy and part of Spain, and eastward to Persia. In the next century, however, much of this was lost. In fact, the Byzantine empire might have disappeared altogether but for the campaigns of Heraclius, its general and later emperor.

Byzantium had too many enemies. The long contest with the forces of Islam, at first the Arabs, later the Turks, began in the seventh century. During this struggle, there were times when Byzantine strength was renewed and the empire expanded, but that only added to the number of enemies pressing on the frontiers. After a heavy defeat by the Seljuk Turks in 1071, Byzantium ceased to be a great power. The walls of Constantinople repelled all attacks until the Ottoman Turks captured the city in 1453, but the empire had shrunk to almost nothing centuries earlier.

Byzantine Civilization

There was no Pope in Constantinople and the emperor was head of the church. Religion and politics therefore could not be separated. That was one reason for the division of Christianity into Western, or Roman, and Eastern, or Orthodox, which became complete in 1054.

Byzantine politics were extremely complicated. People became very passionate about what seem to us small details, although this may be partly due to our lack of understanding. In any case, these internal quarrels seriously weakened the empire.

Byzantine civilization was influenced by many different traditions, from the East as well as the West. In return, Byzantium influenced the West. For example, it is due to the scholars of Constantinople that much of ancient Greek literature has survived. Byzantine scholars were not, however, very interested in new ideas in literature or other fields.

Byzantine art, which is nearly all on religious subjects, shows the effect of the mixing of Eastern and Western influences. A remarkable style developed, which is rather "flat" and almost abstract. People are pictured in surroundings of pure pattern and in brilliant colors. The influence of this style was to be felt as far away as Ireland and, many centuries later, in the painting of El Greco, the great Spanish artist.

The West owed other debts to Byzantium. One of the greatest was to Justinian's code of law; another was to the copiers of ancient manuscripts, whose work was

eventually brought to the West. The fall of Constantinople in 1453 did not mean the end of Byzantine traditions. They continued among the Slav nations, especially the Russians, who had adopted Orthodox Christianity after a sister of the Byzantine Emperor Basil II married Prince Vladimir of Kiev. The glories of Byzantine religious ritual can still be seen in the churches of Moscow and Kiev, while some of the finest Byzantine painting can be found in the churches of Ravenna, Italy.

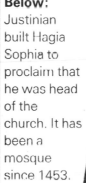

Right: Justinian was the greatest of the Byzantine emperors. He spent many years fighting various enemies, but his greatest achievement was his Code of Law.

Below: Justinian built Hagia Sophia to proclaim that he was head of the church. It has been a mosque since 1453.

Above: A Byzantine icon made from small colored stones or tiles, a form of art called mosaic which was the main form of decoration in Eastern churches for about 1,000 years.

REIGN OF EMPEROR BASIL II 976–1025 • FALL OF CONSTANTINOPLE TO TURKS 1453

THE RISE OF ISLAM

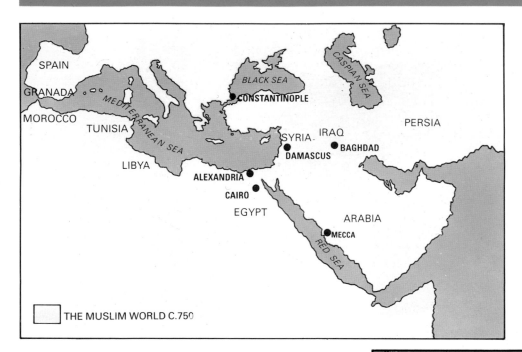

THE MUSLIM WORLD C.750

Left: The teaching of Muhammad inspired the Arabs to set out from their desert homeland to conquer other lands in the name of their religion. For centuries, Europeans felt threatened by the advance of Islam in the east and south.

Below: This lively picture of the Crusaders' attack on Jerusalem was made in the fifteenth century. Of course, Jerusalem did not really have Gothic spires and cathedrals!

A great new power appeared in the world in the seventh century, and it sprang from the deserts of the Arabian peninsula.

Muhammad, who became the founder of a new faith, was at first a religious reformer. His fierce preaching aroused hostility in Mecca, his home town, and, in 622, he and his followers made the *Hejira* (flight) to Medina. This date marks the beginning of the Muslim calendar. Eight years later, Muhammad returned in triumph to Mecca, which contained the Kaaba, the holiest shrine of the Arabs, as it still is for all Muslims throughout the world today. By the time of Muhammad's death only two years later, Arabia was united in the worship of Allah, the one God, and in recognizing Muhammad as his Prophet.

The Arab Conquests

Within a few years, the Arabs had conquered Syria, Iraq, Persia, and Egypt. The conquest was an Arab nationalist movement as well as a religious one, yet it was welcomed in many of the conquered lands, as the Arabs were generally tolerant rulers.

The political and religious head of Islam was the Caliph, and under the Umayyad dynasty, Damascus became his residence. The Umayyad caliphs kept most of the old systems of government and often employed non-Muslims in high positions.

UMAYYAD CALIPHATE (DAMASCUS) 661–750 • ABBASID CALIPHATE (BAGHDAD) 750–1258

In 750, the caliphate was captured by the Abbasids. Their main strength lay in the East, not among the Arabs, and they moved the caliphate to Baghdad. The army, previously dominated by Arabs, became a force of trained slaves, mainly Turkish. The Abbasid caliphate reached its peak under Harun ar-Rashid, who reigned from 786–809, but afterward weakness set in, and eventually the Caliph's rule was restricted to Iraq. Other, independent dynasties were set up in North Africa and Spain. The Fatimids, whose base was Cairo, even captured the city of Baghdad for a short time.

Above: The cool and peaceful arches of the mosque at Cordoba, capital of the most powerful state of Muslim Spain.

Right: A Bedouin of the Arabian desert. From such men came the armies that carried the power of Islam into three continents and made it an international force to rival Christianity.

Islamic Civilization

After their religion, the Arabs' most important gift to Islam was their language, a rich and poetic one. Arabic became the universal language of Islam from Persia to Spain. Muslim law became very complicated in time, but it was simply based on the word of God as revealed to Muhammad in the *Quran* (Koran), the Muslim holy book. The Arabs showed a great ability to learn from different cultural traditions, and Arab scholars made many contributions to mathematics and science. In art and architecture, the Greek, Roman, and Byzantine traditions were transformed into a new, rich style, best seen in the shimmering decoration of mosques. Civilization in Muslim Spain, for example, was, in most ways, far in advance of civilization in Christian Europe.

The Crusades

The Crusades were a series of military expeditions from Europe which set out to regain the Holy Land, which had been taken over by Muslims, for Christianity. The First Crusade (1096–1099) was led by various French lords, including the king of France and the duke of Normandy. They arrived in Constantinople in 1097, crossed Asia Minor, defeated the Seljuk Turks (the dominant Muslim power), and captured the Holy City of Jerusalem in 1099. Although the Byzantine emperor had hoped to regain the territories he had lost to the Muslim powers, in fact, the Crusaders set up states of their own, headed by the kingdom of Jerusalem and guarded by powerful castles.

Muslim Revival

The First Crusade caught the Muslims in a moment of weakness, but the Second Crusade (1147–1149) was a failure. The victories of the great Muslim leader Saladin against the Crusader states resulted in the Third Crusade (1189–1192), in which Richard I of England defeated Saladin, but failed to recapture Jerusalem. The crusading spirit faded and the men of the Fourth Crusade (1202–1204) were principally interested in what they could gain. In 1204 they turned on Constantinople and took many of its treasures.

By 1300 the whole region was securely in Muslim hands. Christian "crusaders" were successful only in Spain, where Granada, the last Muslim state, was conquered in 1492.

FIRST CRUSADE 1096–1099 • SECOND 1147–1149 • THIRD 1189–1192 • FOURTH 1202–1204

MEDIEVAL EUROPE

In the thirteenth century, Europe still looked as nature had made it, with many regions covered by forest or swamp. Society was still divided into those who fought, those who worked, and those who prayed, although a growing number did not fit easily into those categories. Women were either housewives or nuns; few had jobs.

Below left: Among the richest places in late medieval Europe were the city-states of Northern Italy, like Florence and Venice.

THE BLACK DEATH

The terrible disease known as the Black Death swept through Europe in the middle of the fourteenth century, killing thousands. People thought the plague was a punishment from God, and whipped themselves to show how much they regretted their sins.

Towns

Although there were hardly any large cities, towns were growing, and so was trade. Most towns were dominated by an upper class – landowning nobles, rich merchants, or both. Craftsmen and merchants belonged to guilds, which controlled local business and looked after the welfare of their members. Townspeople still made up only a small proportion of the population, but the growth of town life was a sign of the great changes taking place in society.

These changes resulted from the decline of feudalism in western Europe (although not in eastern Europe). Landlords began to let out their land for money rents instead of services, and serfdom was dying out. The decline of feudalism was hastened by a fall in population during the fourteenth century.

One of the causes of this fall was the Black Death, an outbreak of plague which killed about one-third of the European population, far more than any war in history (see the box above). This made labour scarce, resulting in rising wages, prices, and taxes. People began to resent serfdom all the more once it was in decline. In several countries, rebellions broke out, like the Peasants' Revolt in England in 1381. Landlords were attacked, and the clergy too, since they also owned a great deal of land.

HUNDRED YEARS' WAR 1337–1453 • BLACK DEATH 1347–1350 • PEASANTS' REVOLT 1381

Royal Governments

Europeans at this time still had little idea of belonging to a "nation" or "state." Kingdoms were seen as the estate of the king, which might be increased (or reduced) by war or inheritance. Powerful kingdoms did arise in France, England, and Spain, but not, for instance, in Germany or Italy. For a king to create a strong royal government, he had to keep the powerful nobles in check. The French kings had an especially hard job. The part of the kingdom they controlled was small, and it was surrounded by huge estates of great lords (including the king of England), who were loyal to the Crown when it suited them, but disloyal when it did not. Between 1337 and 1453, England and France fought a series of wars over French territory, later known collectively as the Hundred Years' War. The French were finally victorious, thanks partly to the strong leadership of kings like

Philip Augustus, St Louis and Philip the Fair.

The royal government was simply the royal household, although special departments began to develop from the twelfth century. One example was the English Exchequer, or treasury, named after the check tablecloth used to count money on. Local

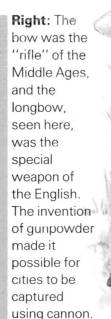

Right: The bow was the "rifle" of the Middle Ages, and the longbow, seen here, was the special weapon of the English. The invention of gunpowder made it possible for cities to be captured using cannon.

officials were in charge of collecting taxes (more important as feudal dues declined) and enforcing the law. It became the custom for kings occasionally to summon assemblies of local representatives. Although we can see in them the beginning of modern parliaments, such assemblies did not make laws. They were simply called together to give information about their home districts, making it easier for the king to collect taxes.

Other signs of the growth of nation states can be seen in the use of local languages in literature. Before the time of Geoffrey Chaucer, author of *The Canterbury Tales* (1340–1400), educated Englishmen usually spoke French (scholars everywhere wrote in Latin). The late Middle Ages was also the time of the last great developments in Gothic art and architecture. Church architecture, the finest artistic achievement of the Middle Ages, became very elegant and delicate, with vast windows of shimmering stained glass.

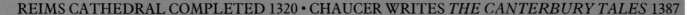

REIMS CATHEDRAL COMPLETED 1320 • CHAUCER WRITES *THE CANTERBURY TALES* 1387

CHINESE CIVILIZATION

A Bronze Age civilization had developed around the Yellow River (Hwang Ho) in China by about 1500 B.C., but the history of China as a unified state does not begin until the Han dynasty, which roughly coincided with the Roman Empire.

Chinese civilization developed over the centuries without sharp or sudden changes. The ideas of Confucius (551–479 B.C.), a Chinese philosopher who taught the importance of a well-ordered life, continued to influence the Chinese until the twentieth century.

A Golden Age

Under the warlike T'ang dynasty, China established a great empire which included Mongolia, Tibet, and Korea. This was a glorious period in Chinese art and literature, as well as a time of prosperity. There were better crops in the fields and the rivers were full of trading boats. Well-planned new towns grew quickly, especially in the south, which was becoming the Chinese heartland. Muslim ships visited Chinese ports, and trade caravans arrived almost daily from Central Asia. The Chinese exported metal goods, porcelain, tea, and silk. They used copper coins which had a hole in the middle so they could be kept on a string. These coins were called *cash*.

Above: Chinese knowledge of crafts like pottery was the envy of other nations. This bowl with painted dragon dates from the Ming dynasty, the last great age of Chinese pottery.

Left: Mongol rulers allowed European merchants to visit China. Marco Polo, here being received with his uncles by Kubilai Khan on his Dragon Throne, stayed in China for almost 20 years.

Right: The Chinese kept their knowledge of silk-making secret. By the seventeenth century there were said to be 50,000 looms like this in the city of Nanking, the capital of Ming China.

T'ANG DYNASTY 618–906 • SUNG 960–1127 (SOUTHERN SUNG 960–1279)

Sung China

The Sung were less warlike than the T'ang, and China was smaller under their rule, but this was another age of artistic brilliance. The wonderful art of Chinese pottery reached its peak at this time, and another Chinese artistic speciality, landscape painting, was established. Some of the finest artists were priests of Buddhism, which had entered China in Han times.

The Sung rulers tried to improve the life of the peasants, although not with much success, as landlords were unwilling to allow them more land. Although they were very poor, Chinese peasants were, however, probably better off than those in Europe at the same time.

China became divided under the Sung, who lost the north, but it was reunited under the Yuan, or Mongol, dynasty, who moved the capital to Beijing. The Mongols had conquered most of Asia, including part of China, early in the thirteenth century under the leadership of Genghis Khan. One of his grandsons, Kubilai Khan, completed the conquest of China in 1279, but had little power beyond its frontiers.

Ming China

The Ming were the last native Chinese dynasty. They restored national unity and economic health, although power remained in the hands of landowners and officials. Since Kubilai Khan, China had been in contact with Europe, and porcelain and silk for European markets was produced in vast amounts. Christian missionaries arrived, bringing clockwork gadgets that fascinated the Chinese, but otherwise Europe had few trade goods that they wanted. Chinese sailors visited the Persian Gulf and East Africa, but the conservative Ming emperors grew hostile to foreign influences. They put a stop to foreign voyaging and restricted European missionaries to the port of Macao, on the southern coast of the country. The emperors of the Manchu (or Ch'ing) dynasty which followed also disliked foreigners, whom they regarded as inferior beings. Pressure from Europeans, who were very eager to trade with the Chinese, however, eventually resulted in the indirect control of Chinese affairs by European powers (see pages 62–63).

YUAN (MONGOL) DYNASTY 1279–1368 • MING 1368–1644 • MANCHU (CH'ING) 1644–1912

JAPANESE CIVILIZATION

Geography had a strong influence on the development of the Japanese. The islands of Japan, 120 miles off the Asian mainland, have never been successfully invaded, so the Japanese never lived under foreign rule. From early times, however, Japan was influenced by China, its great neighbor.

Because the islands of Japan are mountainous, for long periods in the country's history it was difficult for a central government to impose its authority. The Japanese emperor, even if he were descended from the Goddess of the Sun, as was claimed, was no more than a grand puppet, with all the trappings of leadership but none of the power. More important bonds of Japanese society were provided by the strength of family feeling and by religion. The native Japanese religion is Shintoism, which developed from ancient beliefs in nature spirits and the worship of ancestors. Buddhism, introduced from China, became even more influential, especially the form known as Zen.

From the earliest times, Japan was divided up among a number of powerful clans, often at war with each other. One of them was the Fujiwara, which gained control of the emperor in the seventh century and presided over one of the most interesting periods in Japanese history, especially in the arts and literature. One of the most famous (and longest!) novels in the world, *The Tale of Genji*, was written in approximately 1000 by Murasaki Shikibu, a noble lady of the Japanese court.

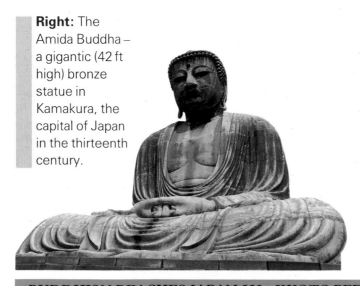

Right: The Amida Buddha – a gigantic (42 ft high) bronze statue in Kamakura, the capital of Japan in the thirteenth century.

The Kamakura Period

From 794–1192, the capital of Japan was Kyoto. Then, in the twelfth century, when the Minamoto clan gained control, it moved to Kamakura. Minamoto Yoritomo, the head of the Minamoto clan, was the first to take the title of shogun and became a kind of military dictator. The warlike spirit of the times was shown by Japan's successful resistance to the Mongols in the late thirteenth century.

The warrior, or samurai, became a favorite subject of literature and painting. These proud, knightly figures also played an important role in society, although they did not always live up to their principles and often added to the general lawlessness caused by the feuds of the land-hungry nobles, or *daimyō*.

The Minamoto shogunate was replaced by the Ashikaga in the fourteenth century, but the Ashikaga shoguns had little control over the constant civil wars in which the people who suffered most were, of course, the peasants, not the knights and nobles responsible for the violence. This period, however, was a golden age for Japanese culture. Landscape gardening and the typically Japanese ceremony of tea drinking developed at this time. So did the *Nō* drama, in which the actors wear masks.

BUDDHISM REACHES JAPAN 552 • KYOTO PERIOD 794–1192 • KAMAKURA PERIOD 1192–1333

Far left: In the late sixteenth and seventeenth centuries, Japanese warlords built stone castles like this one, combining European ideas of fortification with traditional Oriental style. Their old wooden castles had become obsolete since the introduction of guns.

Left: Japanese armor was quite different from medieval European armor. Instead of a steel suit made to fit, the Japanese warrior wore protective pads of iron or leather, which hung from the body on strings. Frightening face masks were also worn.

The Tokugawa Shogunate

Europeans reached Japan in the sixteenth century. They brought, among other things, firearms, which had previously been unknown in Japan. The *daimyō* hastily began building castles of stone (instead of the wood they had previously used), and violence increased. Things, however, were about to change. Three great Japanese heroes were responsible: the general Nobunaga, his lieutenant and successor Hideyoshi, and Ieyasu, who became the first Tokugawa shogun in 1603. Ruling from Edo (Tokyo) the new capital, they rebuilt and reunited Japan, and Ieyasu, having expelled all foreigners, closed down the frontiers. For over 200 years, practically no one was allowed to enter or leave the country. This policy of isolation had many drawbacks, but it had one great advantage: it brought peace to Japan.

ASHIKAGA SHOGUNATE 1338–1568 • CIVIL WAR 1467–1568 • TOKUGAWA SHOGUNATE 1603–1867

INDIAN CIVILIZATION

The oldest religion in India is Hinduism, whose beginnings are lost in time. Its forms of worship are extremely varied, but a common factor is that it divides the whole of society into castes, from Brahmins (priests) at the top to laborers at the bottom. Buddhism also began in India, developing from the teachings of the Buddha, a prince whose real name was Siddhartha Gautama. Like Confucianism, Buddhism is a philosophy of life as well as a religion. It demands the rejection of selfish desires, and brought comfort to people in the lower castes.

Buddhism enjoyed a golden age under Asoka, the great emperor of the Maurya dynasty, who became a Buddhist. Asoka ruled all northern India, including what are now Pakistan and Bangladesh. His government was efficient and remarkably "modern." Records were kept of government business, and censuses were taken of the population. The land was peaceful, and ordinary people enjoyed better lives in Asoka's time than in most other times since. In about 183 B.C., however, the Maurya dynasty was overthrown and warlike nomads invaded northern India.

The Gupta Empire

Indian civilization entered a new and glorious period under the Gupta dynasty, which created an empire stretching right across northern India in the fourth century A.D. The Hindu religion was revived and given new meaning. Literature and the arts flourished, and great advances were made in mathematics. Indian mathematicians invented the system of numbers, from 0 to 10, which was taken up all over the world.

Some of the finest Hindu temples were built in Gupta times. Soaring toward the sky (unlike the Buddhist stupas which cling to the ground), the Hindu temples were covered with carvings, so that they were really sculptures as much as buildings.

Right: The warrior-king Asoka, who became a Buddhist, erected pillars with lion tops (now a symbol of modern India) and writing on the shafts describing Buddhist beliefs and principles of government. The wheel, which also appeared on the columns, is the Buddhist symbol of the law.

DEATH OF BUDDHA c.483 B.C. • MAURYA EMPIRE 321–183 B.C. • DEATH OF ASOKA 232 B.C.

Above: In a curving valley at Ajanta, north-east of Bombay, Buddhist monks turned natural and man-made caves into temples, which in Gupta times were decorated with colorful wall paintings. Ajanta was forgotten for about 1,000 years and rediscovered in the nineteenth century.

The Delhi Sultanate

The Gupta empire began to break up in about 500, under pressure from new invaders from the north-west. Early in the eighth century, Sind (now in Pakistan) was captured by the Arabs. This marked the beginning of a long period of Muslim invasions, and in 1192, a Muslim state known as the Delhi Sultanate was created in the Ganges River valley.

The Delhi Sultanate was not an empire like that of the Guptas, but a collection of small states, some of them Hindu, which were allowed their independence as long as they paid taxes to Delhi. Gradually, the Delhi sultans came to dominate all northern India, but in 1398 Delhi was conquered by the Mongols under Timurlane. The Delhi Sultanate never recovered, and northern India was not reunited until the Mogul dynasty in the sixteenth century.

The Spread of Indian Influence

All these violent changes affected the northern part of the Indian subcontinent. In the south, life was more stable, and Hindu society hardly changed over many centuries. One of the southern kingdoms, founded by the Cholas, created a small empire for itself in the eleventh century, invading the prosperous Buddhist island of Sri Lanka. The Cholas were eventually driven out, but Hindu Tamils (south Indian people) still live in northern Sri Lanka and, sad to say, there is hostility between them and the Sri Lankan Buddhists to this day.

Buddhism eventually almost died out in India, where it was born, but it spread to other countries of East Asia, including China and Japan. The Khmer kingdom of Cambodia, the ruins of whose amazing temples at Angkor can still be seen, was influenced by both the Hindu and Buddhist cultures of India, and "Indianized" kingdoms also grew up in Malaya and Indonesia.

Left: The Ganges River, which flows from the Himalayas through the huge, densely populated plain of northern India, is the great holy river of the Hindus. Pilgrims come to the holy places along the river to bathe in its waters.

RENAISSANCE EUROPE

The Renaissance, or "rebirth", was a time of changing ideas. The word refers to a growing interest in the classical civilizations of ancient Greece and Rome. Through their study of the classics, people came to think more deeply about their own times. They became more interested in the human mind and body and the world around them. Because classical civilization had existed before Christianity, people ceased to believe that the Church had the answer to every question.

Italy

The heart of the Renaissance was in Italy, especially the small, rich city-states of the north such as Florence and Venice. These cities were the leaders of European civilization. They had created the first banks and business companies, and their leading citizens were often merchants and bankers, as well as landowning nobles. These men wanted their cities to look magnificent, with fine palaces and works of art, and they had the money to pay for it. They managed to find an amazing number of brilliant artists to do the work.

The ideas of the Italian Renaissance spread

Below: This figure of a Prophet comes from the vault (ceiling) of the Sistine Chapel in the Vatican in Rome, which was painted by Michelangelo. The total area he painted is about the size of a basketball court!

throughout Europe. It was not, however, all one-way traffic. Northern Europe had much to offer, too. In music and painting (for example, the new art of oil painting), Germany and its neighbors made important contributions. The greatest scholar of the age was Erasmus, a Dutchman. Thanks to the invention of printing with moveable metal type, Erasmus's books were read all over Europe within a few weeks of their being published.

Science and Invention

Renaissance people were interested in everything. Besides painting the *Mona Lisa*, the great artist Leonardo da Vinci dissected human bodies to see how bones and muscles work, and drew plans for all kinds

FIRST PRINTED BOOK (LATIN BIBLE) 1453 • LEONARDO 1452–1519 • ERASMUS 1466–1536

Left: The ideas of the Renaissance spread quickly thanks to the invention of printing with moveable type, which made books cheaper and easier to obtain. Before, books existed only in the form of handwritten documents. Here, Gutenberg, the first successful printer, displays a newly printed page.

Right: Leonardo da Vinci was interested in how things work. This is a page from his notebooks showing his studies of the bones of a human foot, with notes in his back-to-front handwriting.

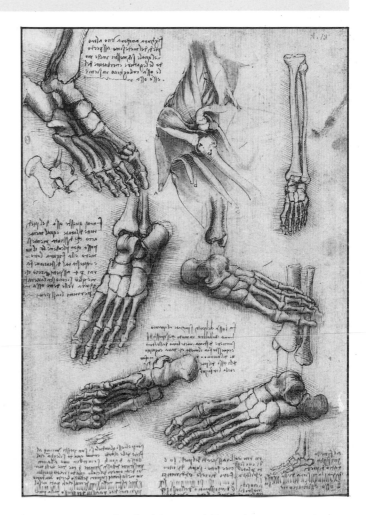

of machines, including what seems to be a helicopter! Andreas Vesalius was a doctor who dissected bodies to learn more about human anatomy. His book on the subject became a bestseller. Nicolaus Copernicus, a Polish-born priest, proved that the earth circles the sun, not (as everyone had thought) the other way around. His book was banned by the Pope because his theories were against the teaching of the church.

As people became more interested in nature, they also began to enjoy it. To a medieval man, a tree might have been useful for its wood, or it might have been a nuisance in the way of the plow, but he never thought of it as something beautiful. The people of the Renaissance admired nature for itself. Gardening became a popular hobby, and Renaissance explorers brought back new plants from the New World, including the potato.

Governments

Politics in the Renaissance were as savage and selfish as ever. New forces were at work in Europe which no one yet fully understood. The first was capitalism, designed to create business and profit (for the capitalists). The second was nationalism. Strong royal governments had appeared in several countries, such as France, Spain, and England, and dynastic rulers were, as ever, keen to increase their lands by marriage or by war. A long-running conflict went on between the Valois (kings of France) and the Hapsburgs (Holy Roman Emperors and kings of Spain), and there was a powerful new ingredient in these wars and conflicts – the Reformation in religion.

COPERNICUS 1473–1543 • MICHELANGELO 1475–1564 • VESALIUS 1514–1564

THE NEW WORLD

The Renaissance spirit of curiosity and inquiry sent European explorers far into the uncharted Atlantic Ocean. Perhaps the greatest of these was Christopher Columbus, an Italian employed by Spain, who sailed westward with three ships in 1492. Curiosity was not the only reason for his voyage. Columbus, like others before and after, was hoping to find a trade route by sea to the Far East, where spices and other luxuries could be bought.

Columbus's idea of reaching the Far East by sailing west seemed a good one. What nobody in Europe knew was that a huge double continent lay across his route. Columbus failed to reach Japan and China, as he had expected. Instead, he discovered the Americas.

Within a few years, the Spaniards had built forts and outposts in the Caribbean and the nearby mainland. Other European nations became interested, and French and English ships, still looking for the westward trade route, touched on the shores of North America. The Americas, however, were not empty of people when they were discovered by Europeans. Mexico and Central and South America were already the home of ancient civilizations.

The Aztecs

The Aztecs were the dominant race in Mexico when the Spaniards arrived. Their capital was Tenochtitlán, a great stone city of nearly 1 million people constructed on an island, where Mexico City is now. The wealth of Tenochtitlán came from heavy taxes paid by other tribes whom the Aztecs had conquered. The

Left: The *Santa Maria* was the largest of Columbus's ships and of the type called a caravel. She was quite sturdy enough for ocean voyages and sailed about as fast as the average modern yacht.

Below: Tenochtitlán was a magnificent city. Its greatest buildings were tall, stepped temples to the gods. At the altar on top, human victims were sometimes sacrificed.

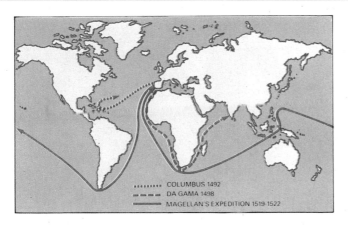

COLUMBUS 1492
DA GAMA 1498
MAGELLAN'S EXPEDITION 1519-1522

Bottom: A ceremonial knife of the Incas, with gold handle in the form of a god. This knife was probably never used, being too precious.

greatest buildings were temples to the Aztec gods, some of whom were very bloodthirsty and demanded human sacrifices. The Aztecs were fine craftsmen in cloth, pottery, jewelry, and stone. They had a form of picture writing, using paper made of leaves, and they lived by a very accurate calendar, based on observation of the sun and stars.

In many ways, Aztec civilization was as advanced as European, but some things were missing. In particular, the American peoples had never made use of the wheel – goods in Mexico were either moved by water or carried by men. Neither did the Aztecs have iron swords or firearms, and they had never seen a horse. As a result, a band of only about 1,000 Spaniards, led by Hernán Cortés, was able to capture Tenochtitlán in 1521, bringing Aztec civilization to a sudden end.

The Incas

The Incas lived 2,400 miles south of the Aztecs and had no contact with them. Their capital was a city called Cuzco and their homeland was Peru, but their empire stretched far to the south. The Incan empire had only existed for about 60 years when it fell in 1534 to 200 Spanish adventurers led by Francisco Pizarro.

The Inca (ruler) himself was a dictator, supported by an aristocratic class and ruling a society in which everyone had his or her appointed place. Incan government was very efficient and, although strict, was fair, even generous. It paid much more attention to the welfare of ordinary people than European governments of the time. Old people, for example, received "pensions" in the form of food. Disabled people were given suitable work: no one was allowed to starve. The laws, however, were strictly enforced and punishments were harsh.

Farming in Peru was more advanced than in Mexico, and the Incas used alpacas and llamas for wool and to transport goods. Incan craftsmen created beautiful metal objects, and buildings were made with such accuracy that the stones fitted together without mortar. Such buildings can still be seen at Machu Picchu, an Incan city high in the Andes Mountains.

Da Gama and Magellan

Soon after Columbus, two Portuguese explorers made other important voyages of discovery. In 1498, Vasco da Gama sailed around Africa to India, and Ferdinand Magellan led the first around-the-world voyage between 1519 and 1522. Although he did not complete the journey himself, one of his ships, the *Victoria*, returned to Spain.

CORTÉS CONQUERS THE AZTECS 1521 • PIZARRO CONQUERS THE INCAS 1534

THE REFORMATION

One sign of the gradual break-up of medieval society was the increasingly poor reputation of the church and the papacy. Having lost much of their religious authority, the Popes tried to make themselves a political power. They built up the Papal States into one of the largest forces in Italy, but that only weakened their authority still more. They then appeared no better than other power-hungry Italian princes.

No one doubted that the church was in serious need of reform. Bishops were often greedy, ambitious men, more interested in worldly luxuries than the kingdom of heaven. Some priests were no better than ignorant louts. (The people of one parish complained that their priest muddled up Jesus and Judas.) The monasteries, once the glory of Christendom, had fallen into a sad state. Monks not only failed to live up to their vows, some even behaved like criminals. Among ordinary people, the religious spirit was very strong, but the church completely failed to satisfy it. As a result of all these problems, demands for reform of the church grew ever louder.

Luther

In 1517, Martin Luther, a German friar and professor of theology, nailed up a list of 95 complaints about church practices (known as the 95 Theses) on a church door in Wittenberg, Germany. He objected chiefly to the selling of papal Indulgences – pieces of paper which promised forgiveness of sins to the people who bought them. Luther did not believe sinners could be forgiven in this way. He believed that this could only happen through the power of God's love, as a result of the personal faith in God of the sinner. At that time Luther did not intend to challenge the authority of the Pope nor the general organization of the church. The Pope, however, replied to his criticisms by excommunicating Luther – that is cutting him off from the church – and this caused a furious argument. As a result, Luther was driven into even stronger opposition. In 1521, a famous debate took place between Luther and his critics at the diet (the name given to the assembly of German princes) at Worms, which was presided over by Charles V, the Holy Roman Emperor, as the church's chief defender. Luther refused to change his views, and from that moment the split in the church became too wide to close.

LUTHER WRITES HIS 95 THESES 1517 • DIET OF WORMS 1521 • PEASANTS' REVOLT 1524

Reformation Germany

Politics as well as religious belief lay behind the Reformation, as the movement for reform in the church became known. Germany was divided into many small states, and there was not a strong central government to protect the peasants from greedy landlords, many of whom were bishops and abbots. Luther thus found many to sympathize with his views, and Lutheran ideas were one of the causes of the Peasants' Revolt (1524), although Luther himself condemned the rebels. At the same time, many rulers saw an advantage in becoming Lutherans because this would rid their lands of the authority of the Pope and clergy and put church property into Lutheran hands.

The Reformation Spreads

Dislike of the clergy and of church authority had its effect in other lands, too. In England, King Henry VIII broke away from the church in Rome and abolished the monasteries, because the Pope would not allow him to divorce Catherine of Aragon, his wife. Henry, however, rejected Lutheran religion, instead making himself head of the Church of England.

The Protestants, as Luther's followers came to be called, were divided among themselves. Huldrych Zwingli, the Swiss reformer, set up a church in Zurich where only God's chosen people (this meant Zwingli's followers) would be "saved." John Calvin, whose

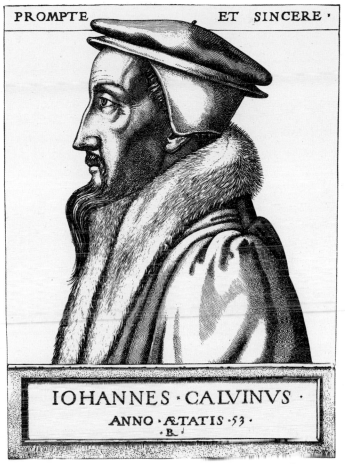

PROMPTE   ET SINCERE·

IOHANNES · CALVINVS ·
ANNO · ÆTATIS ·53·
·B·

church in Geneva was even more strict, was the most influential reformer after Luther.

In 1555, fighting flared up between the Protestant German princes and the Catholic forces of the Emperor Charles V. Later in the same year, a solution of sorts was worked out at the Diet of Augsburg. It was decided that the religion of any German state, Catholic or Protestant, should be left to the ruler.

Left: When Luther put up his 95 Theses, he had no idea that he would start a revolution which would end the universal authority of the medieval church.

Top: The teaching of Calvin led to a stricter form of Protestantism: Calvinists believed they would go to Heaven and everyone else would go to Hell.

HENRY VIII BECOMES HEAD OF THE CHURCH OF ENGLAND 1534 • DIET OF AUGSBURG 1555

MUSLIM EMPERORS

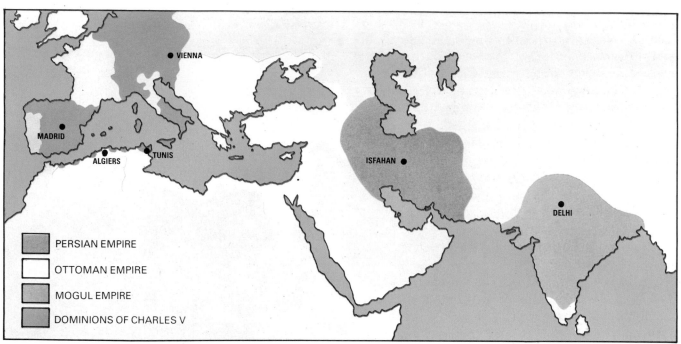

PERSIAN EMPIRE

OTTOMAN EMPIRE

MOGUL EMPIRE

DOMINIONS OF CHARLES V

While Christians expanded into the New World, Islam was expanding in the Old World, and by about 1500 covered a larger area than Christianity. During the sixteenth century, three great Muslim powers flourished, each headed by a ruler of unusual ability.

Persia

Persia, now Iran, was united under the Safavid dynasty, whose subjects considered them the rightful rulers of all Islam. For about a century, the Persians were at war with the Ottoman Turks, but the wars were brought to an end by Shah Abbas the Great, a tolerant ruler who even allowed Christian missionaries into Persia because they encouraged trade. He made Isfahan, the capital, into one of the most beautiful cities in the world, full of mosques and gardens.

The Ottoman Turks

The Ottoman empire was the greatest power in the world in the sixteenth century. The keys to its success were the able rule of the sultans and the power of the army, especially the Janizaries, who were professional soldiers something like the military orders of Christian knights (but supported by the state). In 1453, they conquered Constantinople and for some years there was a real chance that they might overrun Europe. Under Suleiman the Magnificent, they won

Above: In the sixteenth century, three great Muslim empires together dwarfed the Christian dominions of Charles V, the Holy Roman Emperor.

Right: Europeans, impressed by Suleiman's splendid court, called him "the Magnificent." His own people called him "the Law-giver."

OTTOMAN EMPIRE c.1300–1922 • SAFAVID DYNASTY 1502–1736 • MOGUL EMPIRE 1526–1858

Hungary in 1525, and attacked, but did not capture, Vienna. The Ottoman empire was governed better, and with greater tolerance, than most Christian countries. Suleiman's grand vizier (chief minister) had been a Christian slave and the former subjects of Constantinople were allowed to continue to worship as Orthodox Christians.

There were weaknesses in the Ottoman empire, especially economic ones. Capitalism never developed to create new wealth. Also, the Ottomans were a land power by tradition, and, although they built up a navy, they were defeated by a combined Christian fleet at the Battle of Lepanto in 1571. They never fully recovered from this disaster, although Ottoman sultans continued to rule Turkey until 1922.

Mogul India

The Moguls were a Muslim dynasty of Mongol origin, who founded an empire in northwest India in 1526. Although it was won by force, the Mogul empire was maintained by good government. As Muslims ruling a largely Hindu population, the Moguls were tolerant in religious matters. Akbar, perhaps the greatest Mogul ruler, liked to talk with people of different beliefs. He loved learning, literature, and the arts and kept an extremely luxurious court.

The Moguls produced some of the most beautiful buildings the world has ever seen, including the Taj Mahal. Mogul court art, in which Indian and Persian traditions mingled, was no less magnificent, and crafts like metalwork and rug-making reached high levels.

Akbar's successors grew less tolerant, spent too much money (on wars as well as courtly luxury), and made more enemies, especially the Mahrattas in central India. The Emperor Aurangzeb held the empire together between 1658 and 1707, but was constantly at war. Under his successors, central government broke down and India was divided again into small, warring states. In 1738, Nadir Shah, last of the great Muslim conquerors, who had already overthrown the Safavids in Persia, sacked Delhi with horrible cruelty. There was not a power left at the center, but already the Europeans were established in many places. By 1763, for example, the greatest power in India was the British East India Company, which had been set up for trade, but which became increasingly political.

Right: Under Shah Abbas, Persia (Iran) reached the height of its power and prestige. Persian arts, including the famous carpets, were at their finest.

Above: The Taj Mahal was built in white marble, as a memorial to the wife of the Mogul Emperor Shah Jahan.

REIGN OF SULEIMAN 1520–1566 • REIGN OF AKBAR 1556–1605 • REIGN OF ABBAS 1586–1628

WARS OF RELIGION

The Roman Catholic Church fought back against the Protestant Reformation (see pages 42–43). Among the "weapons" of this Counter Reformation were the Inquisition, especially in Spain, which sought out and often executed anyone who was not deemed to be a good Catholic, and the Jesuits, members of a new religious order, who were most active in education and as missionaries. The religious divisions also played a large part in European wars.

France

Although France remained Catholic, there were a large number of Protestants, known as Huguenots, in the population, including noble families. A series of savage civil wars were fought between the two groups, but the worst incident happened during a truce. The Catholic party, led by the Duke of Guise, plotted to kill the Huguenot leaders on St. Bartholomew's Day, August 24, 1572. Events got out of hand, the Catholic mob in Paris joined in, and thousands of Huguenots were murdered. Finally, in 1589, Henry of Navarre, a Huguenot, inherited the throne. Although he became a Catholic, his Edict of Nantes in 1598 made the Huguenot religion legal.

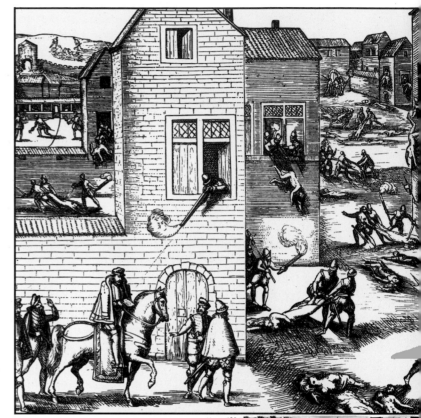

The Netherlands

The Netherlands was one of the most advanced nations in Europe. It became Protestant during its struggle against Spain, which, besides being the leading Catholic state, ruled the Dutch. Inspired by William the Silent, Prince of Orange, the seven northern provinces of the Netherlands (including Holland), declared their independence in 1579. In spite of many defeats and the murder of William the Silent in 1584, the Dutch continued their fight until Spain signed a truce in 1609. This marked the beginning of the Dutch republic.

The Armada

The Dutch received some help from the Protestant English, who were on bad terms with Spain, thanks partly to the raids of privateers like Francis Drake on the Spanish colonies in the Americas. Philip II, the Spanish king, planned to crush the English for good, and in 1588 sent the Armada, a large invasion fleet, against them. Aided by the weather, the English chased it away, around the north coast of Scotland and back to Spain.

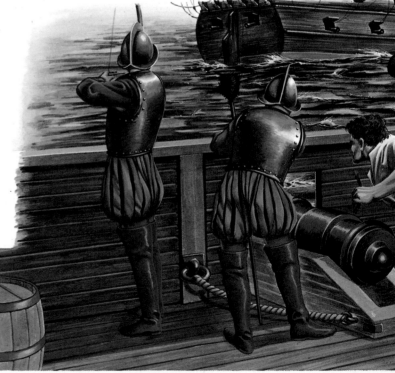

FRENCH RELIGIOUS WARS 1562–1598 • DUTCH REVOLT AGAINST SPAIN 1568–1609

Left: French Catholic leaders killed Admiral Coligny and other Huguenot leaders on the night before St Bartholomew's Day, while they were gathered in Paris for the wedding of Henry of Navarre.

The Thirty Years' War

A war (or, more accurately, series of wars) in which religion played some part, took place mainly in Germany from 1618–1648. It began as a civil war within the Holy Roman Empire between the Protestant princes and the Catholics backed by Spain and Austria, both ruled by the Hapsburg dynasty. Other countries, afraid of growing Hapsburg power, aided the Protestants, whose most useful ally was Gustavus Adolphus, king of Sweden, a brilliant general. Later, even Catholic France joined Protestant Sweden for the same reason.

Power, not religion, had become the chief motive for war. Most of Europe eventually became involved, and by the time the war ended, with the Peace of Westphalia in 1648, it had become clear that the mighty Hapsburg power was in decline, and the most powerful nation in Europe was France.

European Prosperity

In spite of wars, western Europe grew richer in the seventeenth century. The population was rising as a result of improvements in farming. Trade was increasing, too, assisted by banks and capitalist business methods such as "joint-stock" companies, in which money was raised by selling stocks and shares. Industry was still for the most part organized in craftsmen's workshops, but, helped by the demands of war, mining and engineering were developing fast.

In eastern Europe, there was less change. There, the old feudal system continued.

Left: King Philip II of Spain was the leader of Roman Catholic Europe, and England was the largest Protestant kingdom. That was one reason for his attempt to invade England in 1588. Although English guns could not sink the Spanish galleons, the Armada was scattered.

SPANISH ARMADA SENT AGAINST ENGLAND 1588 • THIRTY YEARS' WAR 1618–1648

AN AGE OF ABSOLUTISM

Most people in about 1600 agreed that their government had supreme power over them. As governments were usually headed by kings, there was, in theory, no limit to royal authority. The day-to-day business of government was generally carried out by paid officials, who themselves depended on the king. In practice, however, the king was not all-powerful. The main check on his power was his need for money. This could only come from taxes, and if taxes were too high, rebellion was likely.

Louis XIV

The greatest king in Europe at this time was undoubtedly the king of France. France was the largest, richest, and most powerful state, and Louis XIV acted as if it were his private property. He lived in a magnificent new palace at Versailles, surrounded by great nobles who were little more than obedient courtiers. The king's word was law, even on questions of religion.

Louis' ambitions and the fear of France among lesser states caused a succession of wars. Although France had a superb army and a strong economy, by about 1700 war was beginning to drain the country's strength away.

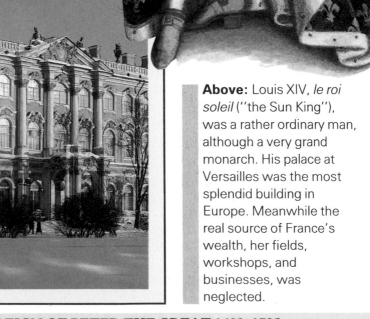

RUSSIA

The state of Russia began in the Middle Ages as a group of Slav tribes brought together under the dukes of Muscovy, who later became czars (emperors) of Russia.

In 1682, Peter the Great became czar. Russia was then the most backward country in Europe, and Peter set out to modernize it by bringing in knowledge, technology, and trade from the more advanced countries to the west. He built a new capital at St. Petersburg, on the Baltic Sea, which made contact with the West easier. (The Winter Palace, shown on the right, was built there some years later.)

Russian power increased under Peter and his successors. By defeating Sweden in the Great Northern War, Peter made Russia the most important country in the north. Under Catherine the Great, who ruled from 1762–1796, Russia gained control of the Black Sea and seized part of Poland.

Above: Louis XIV, *le roi soleil* ("the Sun King"), was a rather ordinary man, although a very grand monarch. His palace at Versailles was the most splendid building in Europe. Meanwhile the real source of France's wealth, her fields, workshops, and businesses, was neglected.

REIGN OF LOUIS XIV 1643–1715 • REIGN OF PETER THE GREAT 1682–1725

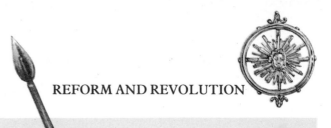

England

In England, too, the king claimed to have no superior except God, but his authority was somewhat restricted by the growing power of parliament. Quarrels between Charles I and parliament over religion and money ended in civil war in 1642. The parliamentary forces, under the leadership of Oliver Cromwell, were victorious and the king was executed in 1649. Although the monarchy was restored in 1660, King James II, a Catholic, was expelled in 1688. The English then invited William of Orange, a Dutch Protestant, to take the Crown.

The Dutch

After gaining independence from Spain, the United Provinces (as the Dutch state was then called) became

Right: A soldier in Oliver Cromwell's New Model Army. These soldiers were called Roundheads because they cut their hair short, unlike the long-haired Cavaliers, or Royalists.

Left: The Dutch had no splendid monarch, but were as proud of themselves as any French nobleman. In this painting, a mayor listens to the troubles of an old woman.

the first country in Europe to break away from the old system of government by a hereditary monarch. Power was divided between the States General, an assembly representing merchants and bankers, and the Stadtholder, usually the head of the house of Orange.

The Dutch were the most prosperous people in Europe. Most of their wealth came from ships and trade, and their success aroused the jealousy of England, which despite being their natural ally was also, at sea, their chief rival. A series of naval wars for supremacy at sea were fought between the Dutch and the English (see below right), but the alliance was renewed when William of Orange became king of England in 1688.

The Spanish Succession

A greater danger to the Dutch was France, and William became the leader of a European alliance to limit French power. Danger threatened when, because the king of Spain did not have any children, it seemed likely that France would become united with Spain. To prevent this, the war of the Spanish Succession (1702–1713) was fought. This was the last of Louis XIV's wars, as the apparently unbeatable French armies were finally defeated. It was also the first of a series of European wars in which France and England (united with Scotland since 1707) were on opposite sides, as they competed vigorously to become the world's dominant power.

ENGLISH CIVIL WAR 1642–1645 • ENGLISH-DUTCH WARS 1652–1654, 1665–1667, 1672–1674

AMERICAN INDEPENDENCE

Below: The first English colonists in Massachusetts were religious refugees. They traded with the Indians, who also taught them how to grow new crops.

In the 200 years following the discovery of the Americas, European colonies there grew enormously. Spanish territory stretched from California to Chile, and although most of it contained few people, Mexico City became one of the largest cities in the world.

Spanish settlement had a dreadful effect on the native inhabitants. Some races were wiped out by European violence or European diseases, and everywhere the population fell sharply. Because workers were in short supply, the Spaniards, along with other colonizing nations, imported captured Africans as slaves to work in the sugar and tobacco plantations the Spaniards had established. This terrible trade in human beings went on until the nineteenth century.

The English Colonies

By comparison with the Spanish empire, with its large silver mines, North America seemed a poor land. Apart from furs and fish it seemed to have little to offer merchants and businessmen. The Europeans who settled here (many of them religious refugees), however, soon found other things of value, such as good farming land. By 1700, about 500,000 Europeans lived along the East Coast. They included Dutch, French, Swedes, and others, but the greatest number were English. By 1732, there were 13 colonies from Maine to Georgia, all with royal governors appointed in London, but their own assemblies, and all enjoying a large degree of democracy and freedom.

FIRST ENGLISH COLONY IN AMERICA 1607 • SEVEN YEARS' WAR 1756–1763

The Seven Years' War

This war, which lasted from 1756–1763, was the greatest of the European conflicts in the eighteenth century. It was fought both in Europe and in other continents where European nations competed for trade. In Europe, it was notable for the successful resistance of Prussia, a new power, against a combination of continental enemies. Abroad, it resulted in the victory of the British over the French, enabling them to become the world's dominant sea power. In particular, the British won Bengal in India in 1757 and gained control over the French provinces in Canada after capturing Quebec in 1759. British victory in Canada meant that the regions which belonged to the British Hudson Bay Company there and the 13 British colonies in America were no longer separated by the French and in danger of being cut off. This huge North American empire, however, did not last long.

The American Revolution

The American colonies were not very popular with the British government. Colonies were supposed to supply cheap raw materials and to buy the manufactured products of the mother country, but the colonists had their own industries, such as shipbuilding. The colonists also resented paying British taxes. When the British government tried to make the colonists pay more taxes, the colonists replied that they should not pay taxes at all unless they had their own representatives in the British parliament. In 1773, when the British imposed a new tax on tea, some colonists dressed as Indians and boarded three tea ships in Boston harbor. Then, in a gesture of protest, they threw the cargo overboard. This event later became known as the Boston Tea Party. There were other quarrels. The colonists wanted the freedom to expand to the West, but the government, foreseeing trouble with the Indians, tried to prevent them.

In 1775, war finally broke out and in 1776, the American colonists declared their independence. The British sent two armies against them, but both were defeated by the skilful colonial fighters, with some help from the French. The Constitution of the United States of America was drawn up in 1787. It created a federal system of government, with a president and congress for the whole country, as well as elected state governments responsible for local matters. This was the first written document which laid down the rules for the government of a country. By recognizing that all citizens (slaves were not counted) had equal rights, this was also the first time a government recognized that the state exists for the benefit of its citizens. In 1789, George Washington, who had led the American forces against the British, was chosen as the first president.

Right: In a famous episode during the War of Independence, Washington, who had been in full retreat, crossed the Delaware River to attack the British in New Jersey on Christmas Eve, 1776.

WAR OF INDEPENDENCE 1775–1783 • WASHINGTON BECOMES FIRST US PRESIDENT 1789

THE FRENCH REVOLUTION

In the eighteenth century, under the rule of Louis XVI, France seemed to be a grand and glorious country. Her government, however, was incapable, unfair and bankrupt. Society was in great need of change.

The influence of the American Revolution and the ideas of freedom and equality stirred up by French writers such as Voltaire and Rousseau helped to raise people's hopes. In 1789, the government of King Louis XVI was forced to call the Estates General, which contained representatives of the middle class as well as clergy and nobles. They declared themselves a National Assembly, which represented the power of the people, not the state.

This assembly carried out a revolution in government. Politics and law were reformed. The special privileges of nobles and clergy were swept away. All men were declared equal. Never has a society been changed so thoroughly in so short a time.

These dramatic changes, however, were not carried out without violence. The guillotine claimed many lives, including those of the king and his wife, Marie Antoinette. War broke out with other European

REVOLUTION BEGINS JULY 1789 • LOUIS XVI AND MARIE ANTOINETTE GUILLOTINED 1793

powers, but France's new army of "citizens and brothers" defeated the experienced, professional soldiers of Austria and Prussia.

The French Revolution had a lasting effect on the whole of Europe. The ideas of liberty, equality and brotherhood, were international. They had many supporters in other countries, although not usually among governments, which felt threatened by them. Modern European politics, with its division between liberals and conservatives, dates from this time.

The Emperor

The French Revolution ended in the dictatorship of Napoleon Bonaparte, a strong leader and brilliant general. In 1804, he made himself emperor.

Napoleon's greatest gift to France was the new legal system known as the *Code Napoléon*. His conquests carried the *Code* – and the Revolutionary ideas of equality and freedom – into other countries.

By 1808, Napoleon controlled most of Europe, although his attempt to invade Britain had been thwarted at the Battle of Trafalgar, which took place at sea in 1805. In 1812, he invaded Russia, but although he won a close victory at Borodino, his army of 600,000 men was almost destroyed during the long march home.

Napoleon surrendered in 1814, and was sent to the island of Elba, but he escaped to fight one last campaign. It ended in his defeat at the Battle of Waterloo in 1815. This time he was sent further away, to the island of St. Helena in the South Atlantic, where he died in 1821.

In France, the monarchy regained power, and conservative statesmen restored the European frontiers of 1788. The ideas of the French Revolution, however, could not be suppressed.

Above left: Marie Antoinette, doomed queen of Louis XVI.

Left: On July 14, 1789, workers of Paris captured and destroyed the Bastille, a royal fortress.

Right: Napoleon was not only a good general and an intelligent and energetic man, he was also an inspired leader and remained loyal to most of the best ideas of the Revolution.

BATTLE OF TRAFALGAR 1805 • BATTLE OF BORODINO 1812 • BATTLE OF WATERLOO 1815

MACHINES AND FACTORIES

The most important change in history since farming began was the Industrial Revolution of the nineteenth century. Western society was changed for ever.

The most obvious feature of the Industrial Revolution was the change in the way goods were made. Instead of being produced individually by craftsmen in workshops, goods were mass-produced by machines in factories. Perhaps the most important feature, however, was the speed at which change began to take place. During the Middle Ages, life hardly changed over the centuries. Someone who lived in the twelfth century, for example, would have been quite at home if he or she had been born again in the fifteenth. But someone who lived at the beginning of the nineteenth century would have been completely bewildered by life at the beginning of the twentieth. This increased speed of change has continued to this day, and shows no sign of slowing down.

The Right Conditions

Huge economic changes can only take place when the conditions are right. In the eighteenth century, trade increased enormously, making profits which could be invested. Farming also improved, thanks to more scientific methods. This resulted in more food and a growing population. Therefore, two essentials – capital and labor (money and workers) – were present.

Power and Machines

A third element was needed to make the revolution possible and that was new technology, machines that would do a job 100 times faster than human hands. The power to drive these new machines came from coal and from steam engines. More coal was produced mainly by employing more miners, but a useful industrial steam engine did not exist until one was invented by James Watt, a Scottish engineer, in 1769. Coal and steam also provided the power to make iron and steel

Right: When England became an industrial society, it had to be able to produce food for the masses of factory workers. Before the advance in industry came an advance in farming, with machines like Jethro Tull's seed drill – a great improvement on sowing by hand.

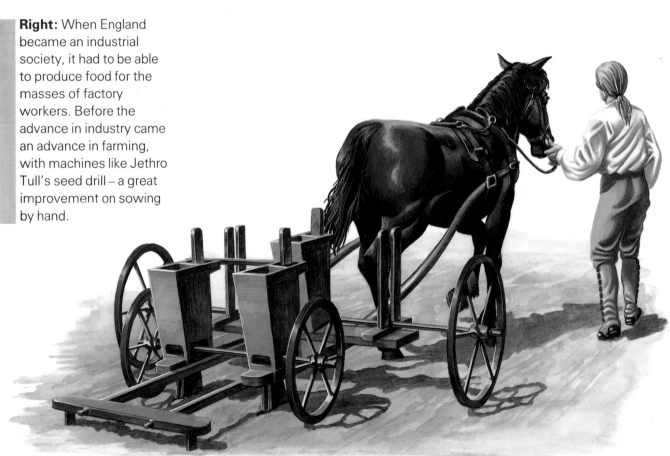

TULL'S SEED DRILL INVENTED 1701 • HARGREAVES' SPINNING JENNY INVENTED 1764

for use in heavy industry of all kinds.

Now that there was a use for machines, they were invented thick and fast, as one invention sparked off another. For example, soon after James Hargreaves invented the spinning jenny, which mechanized the spinning process, Edmund Cartwright invented the power loom, which made weaving faster, too.

The new, power-driven machines made it necessary to gather all the workers in one place – a factory. There, people learned a new way of working. They had to keep regular hours and work at a steady pace, to keep up with the machines. Managers and foremen kept a close watch on the workers.

Below: The first British industry to use steam-driven machines was the textile industry.

Below right: A British certificate of trade union membership.

Industrial Society

In the new industrial regions, large smoky cities grew up. They were not properly planned, and the workers were crowded into slums with no running water. The factories were noisy and dangerous. People, including children, worked 12 hours a day for low wages, with no vacations and no insurance against illness or unemployment. A Frenchman visiting Manchester, England, exclaimed in horror that people were being turned back into savages.

None of the horrors of industrial society was entirely new. For example, small children worked equally long hours on farms. What was new was the size of the problem – the dirty, ever-growing cities, and the masses of poor workers crowded into them.

By the second half of the nineteenth century, politicians had begun to realize that something had to be done. Laws were passed to limit working hours and control housing conditions. Proper drains and sewers were built. Trades unions were allowed in Britain and some employers began to understand that they could pay decent wages without lowering their profits.

8 HOURS LABOUR!

NATIONAL UNION of GAS WORKERS & GENERAL LABOURERS OF GREAT BRITAIN AND IRELAND

This is to Certify that

WATT'S STEAM ENGINE INVENTED 1769 • CARTWRIGHT'S POWER LOOM INVENTED 1785

THE RAILROAD AGE

In the early nineteenth century, the fastest ways to travel were on horseback or by ship. It took about two weeks for news from Italy to reach England, over a month for it to reach New York. Transport was not only slow, it was expensive, and the Industrial Revolution would have been impossible without faster and cheaper methods.

Canals and Roads

The first step was to make better use of the methods that existed already. Most eighteenth-century roads were terrible. One traveler fell off his horse into a pothole so deep that he drowned. In the early nineteenth century, better ways of making roads were invented, along with better coaches. A journey that took seven days by stage coach in 1730 took only 17 hours by mail coach in 1830.

Bulky goods traveled by water, but rivers did not always flow smoothly, or in the right place. In the late eighteenth century, however, barge traffic increased enormously as a result of the construction of canals.

Railroads

These improvements were impressive, but they were soon made obsolete by the building of railroads. Carts drawn by horses had run on wooden rails in mines since the sixteenth century, but a modern railroad needed iron rails that would not break and a locomotive that would pull a train. The invention of the steam locomotive by Richard Trevithick in 1804, and other technological advances, made both these things possible by 1830, and all that was required then was money to pay for railroad construction.

The importance of railroad companies was quickly recognized and people proved eager to invest in them. They provided a stimulus to other industries, not only to the iron and steelmaking industries which provided rails and rolling stock, but equally to enterprises which depended on quick and cheap transport. For example, deposits of coal or mineral ores which had been too far away to make them worth mining were suddenly brought within easy reach.

Left: The first "steam locomotives" were road vehicles, like this one which ran in England, although it was never a regular service. The rough surface caused too many mechanical breakdowns, and steam carriages soon disappeared.

Roads and Ships

For carrying goods or passengers, the railroads had no rivals until the invention of the internal combustion engine (the engine that drives most motor vehicles) in the late nineteenth century. In 1905, Henry Ford began making the Model T Ford, the first family car, by mass production (it took only 63 minutes to produce each car). The roads, which had become almost deserted since the railroads arrived, soon began to fill up again.

The steam engine, which had been put to such good use in the locomotive, also provided the power for much faster, larger, more reliable ships, and iron and steel replaced wood for ships' hulls. The new ships had some drawbacks. They needed coal, and coaling stations had to be built all around the world, but the building of the Suez and Panama Canals (opened in 1869 and 1914 respectively) shortened shipping routes by thousands of miles.

Left: A locomotive from an early British railroad.

Right: A Model T Ford, the first mass-produced motor car.

COMMUNICATIONS

During the nineteenth century, postal services improved very dramatically. Railroads allowed much cheaper and faster postal deliveries, and by the end of the century, the European postal system was as quick as it is today.

Faster communications were provided by the electric telegraph, which was invented by Samuel Morse in 1835. It had connected most big cities by 1870. Faster still was the telephone, patented by Alexander Graham Bell in 1876. The first telephone exchange was operating in 1877, although telephones did not become common until after 1918. Among other results of these fast methods of communication was the rise of the modern newspaper industry.

A BRITISH PENNY BLACK STAMP

AN ELECTRIC TELEGRAPH

AN EARLY TELEPHONE

THE AMERICAN CIVIL WAR

In 1800, the USA was a small country of about 5 million people all living in a strip of land along the East Coast. The purchase of huge stretches of land from France, Spain, and Russia, and the taking of more land by force (especially from Mexico), enabled the country to reach almost its present size by 1867.

The population and the economy of the country grew along with its boundaries. This was, however, a divided society. The biggest division was between the North, a land of towns and factories, and the South, a land of farms, especially large cotton plantations. (Cotton provided more than half of total US exports in 1860.) The workers in the plantations were slaves of African descent and Southerners believed that slavery was necessary if they were to continue to make their living. Most Northerners, however, were opposed to the existence of slavery.

Civil War

In 1860, Abraham Lincoln was elected president. He was the candidate of the Republican Party, which opposed slavery. The Southern states therefore withdrew from the Union. Lincoln's government declared that they had no right to do so, and the result was the Civil War (1861–1865).

The North had more men, money, and machines and an established government. It also controlled the sea and could therefore prevent aid from reaching the South from other countries. Although the Southerners, or Confederates, fought with great determination, they were defeated and surrendered in April 1865. Five days later Lincoln was assassinated. With the Emancipation Proclamation in 1863, Lincoln had made slavery, the immediate cause of the war, illegal, and the victory of the Union (the North) ensured that the USA remained a single nation.

Westward Ho!

With the Union safe, the USA expanded and grew prosperous (see also pages 64–65). Immigrants from many parts of Europe, mostly poor people seeking a better life, poured in at the rate of 1,000 a week. Some stayed in cities in the East, others moved on across the mountains. The huge territories in the West began to fill up rapidly as settlers followed in the footsteps of the fur traders, pioneers, and cattle ranchers who had gone before them.

ABRAHAM LINCOLN ELECTED PRESIDENT 1860 • AMERICAN CIVIL WAR 1861–1865

Land of Opportunity

The USA was the land of democracy, freedom, and riches – but not for everyone! The booming cities contained masses of poor workers. The blacks, although no longer slaves, were little better off than they had been. They had little chance of success in white society, neither in the farmlands of the South, where they were tenants dependent on white landlords, nor in the industrial cities of the North, where they were underpaid and exploited. The native Indians received even worse treatment. White settlers took the Indians' land, and professional hunters, like "Buffalo Bill" Cody, slaughtered the bison which had been the Indians' source of meat. Bitter wars were fought against Indian nations like the Cheyenne and the Sioux, who were crowded into reservations (land the white settlers did not want), where their culture slowly became less important.

Above: Russian immigrants arriving in New York City. In the nineteenth century, the USA had huge amounts of land and few people. Immigrants from poor European countries were welcome.

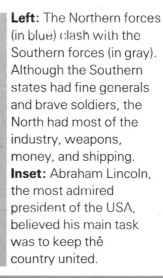

Left: The Northern forces (in blue) clash with the Southern forces (in gray). Although the Southern states had fine generals and brave soldiers, the North had most of the industry, weapons, money, and shipping.
Inset: Abraham Lincoln, the most admired president of the USA, believed his main task was to keep the country united.

EMANCIPATION PROCLAMATION 1863 • ABRAHAM LINCOLN ASSASSINATED 1865

AFRICAN CIVILIZATIONS

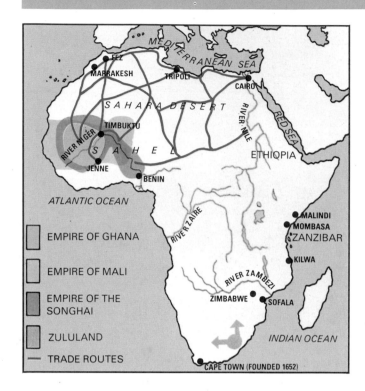

EMPIRE OF GHANA

EMPIRE OF MALI

EMPIRE OF THE SONGHAI

ZULULAND

— TRADE ROUTES

Above: Until the nineteenth century, Europeans knew little of Africa, but great empires existed centuries earlier.

Right: The ruins of Great Zimbabwe. The brick walls and tower were built in about the sixteenth century, but this was an important place 400 years earlier.

These little states, including Kilwa and Zanzibar, developed their own Afro-Arab culture and the people there spoke Swahili, a new language. Further south and inland was the state of Zimbabwe, whose wealth was derived from the gold trade. The state was centered on a complex of stone buildings, the largest of which date from about 1500. We know very little about ancient Zimbabwe, except that it was destroyed by the Zulu in the early nineteenth century.

West Africa
Ghana disappeared in the thirteenth century, but the larger empire of Mali soon grew up in the same region. This new empire accepted Islam, and under Muslim rule, Timbuktu, one of its principal towns, became a center of learning and education. The rulers of Mali were in turn overthrown by one of their sub-

ject peoples, the Songhai, who established an even greater empire in the fifteenth century. Songhai control of the rich Saharan trade eventually provoked an attack by the sultan of Morocco in 1591, and their empire was destroyed. It was never restored.

In some ways, civilization was more advanced further east. The state of Benin (eastern Nigeria) flourished from the fourteenth to the seventeenth century. It was particularly notable for its sculpted bronze and terracotta heads and figures, which can still be seen in many museums throughout the world. A seventeenth-century Dutch traveler thought that the capital of Benin was as fine a city as the Dutch capital of Amsterdam.

In ancient times, North Africa belonged to the Mediterranean world. Although cut off from black Africa by the Sahara Desert, there was always contact between the north and the people of the Sahel, south of the desert. Berbers from North Africa founded the kingdom of Ghana (northwest of modern Ghana) in the fourth century A.D., and trade routes crossed the Sahara, carrying salt from the north and gold from the south.

East Africa
The Nile River provided another route south. In the fourth century, it brought a Syrian missionary to Ethiopia, and the country became and remained Christian, in the middle of a largely Muslim region, until this century.

Muslim traders from the Red Sea and the Persian Gulf founded city-states along the East African coast.

Left: The mosque at Jenne, northern Nigeria. Christianity was brought to coastal regions by Europeans. Islam spread southward from North Africa.

The Slave Trade

Europeans began to set up trading posts on the coast of West Africa in the fifteenth century. As time went by, the chief item of trade came to be slaves – African men, women, and children captured in war and sold to Europeans. Between 1700 and 1800 about 7 million people were carried across the Atlantic to work as slaves in the USA. Besides the misery inflicted on the slaves themselves, this dreadful business wrecked African society, making warfare and kidnapping a way of life.

Colonial Africa

The slave trade ended in the nineteenth century, but European interest in Africa did not. Most of the continent was still almost completely unknown to Europeans, but a few colonies had been founded. The most important of these was the Dutch colony in South Africa based on Cape Town. As the Dutch settlers, who came to be known as Boers (farmers), went further into African land, they came into conflict with the Zulu, who had formed a powerful, warlike kingdom, and the British, who had taken over the Dutch colony in 1814. In the end, the Zulu were defeated and the Boers gained large new territories, but lost their independence to the British in the Boer War, which ended with the Treaty of Vereeniging.

European rivalries led to the "Scramble for Africa" at the end of the nineteenth century. Although European governments had no great desire to own vast colonies in Africa, they did not want their rivals to own them either, and so by the end of the century all of Africa was under European control, except Ethiopia.

Left: Trade across the Sahara Desert probably existed even in prehistoric times. After the camel was introduced over 1,500 years ago, travel became easier.

ZULU WAR 1879 • BOER WAR 1899–1902 • PEACE OF VEREENIGING 1902

THE POWER OF THE WEST

During the nineteenth century, the West (that is Europe and the USA) came to dominate the world. In some parts, such as almost all of Africa, Western control took the form of direct colonial rule. In other parts, Europe's economic and military power compelled foreign governments to follow policies which suited the West. On the whole, the European "conquest" was carried out with little need for military force, thanks to the naval strength of Great Britain, the richest and most powerful European state.

Below: In India, a country with a long history of luxurious courts, the British governed with much ceremony. This is the Durbar (a state reception) of the British viceroy, at Delhi in 1902.

The British Empire

London was the center of the world economy in the nineteenth century, and sterling was the chief currency. British investment provided the capital for industrial development in the USA and other countries, while the industrialization of Russia was carried out largely with French capital. The British were strong supporters of the principle of free trade, as they produced cheaper goods than other countries.

The British Empire was enormous. It included Australia and New Zealand, which had been discovered and claimed for Britain in the late eighteenth century by Captain James Cook, and the other white dominions (as they came to be called) of Canada and South Africa. Also part of the Empire was India and, by 1900, many countries in Africa and elsewhere in Asia. It was not the colonies themselves that made Britain rich, however, but manufacturing and trade.

OPIUM WAR 1839–1842 • TAIPING REBELLION 1850–1864 • SINO-JAPANESE WAR 1894–1895

Right: A wooden carving of a European missionary, made in tropical Africa in the nineteenth century.

South America

Most countries of Latin America won independence in the early nineteenth century under inspiring leaders like Simon Bolívar (1783–1830). Healthy development in the new republics, however, was spoiled by civil wars and poor economic resources. Mexico, declared a republic in 1826, was later forced to surrender more land to the USA, following the Mexican War (1846–1848). The USA regarded Latin America as its "backyard" and in 1823 formulated the Monroe Doctrine. This important principle of US foreign policy stated that no interference in the Western Hemisphere by European powers would be allowed.

Below: A statue of Simon Bolívar in Caracas, Venezuela. He swore not to rest until Spanish rule in South America ended.

The Far East

Trade with China had always been difficult because Europe did not have a product the Chinese wanted, but at last one was found – the drug opium. It took a brief war to force China into the world trade pattern, as a result of which the British gained Hong Kong, their own commercial colony in China. Meanwhile, Russia took advantage of China's weakness to seize lands in the north. These troubles aggravated China's own problems, which came to a head in the Taiping Rebellion (1850–1864) and military defeat by Japan. In spite of some overdue reforms, the last Manchu emperor, a boy, was forced to abdicate in 1911.

Japan was also forced to open its doors to aggressive western businessmen – the Americans in this case. The last Tokugawa shogun resigned and the emperor's powers were restored. Like the Chinese, the Japanese saw they could only resist western influence by adopting western ways, but they were more successful in doing so. The rising power of Japan was displayed by its defeat of China and, more surprisingly, of Russia in 1905.

In Southeast Asia, the Dutch established colonial control of Indonesia (Vietnam, Cambodia, and Laos). In the Philippines, a nationalist rebellion against Spanish rule ended in domination by the USA.

SOUTH AMERICAN WARS OF LIBERATION 1810–1825 • MEXICAN WAR 1846–1848

PEACE AND PROSPERITY

In the 100 years after the defeat of Napoleon, Europe suffered fewer wars than in any other century, and the wars that *were* fought were small ones. From 1870 especially, European nations were growing faster than ever before, and their extra population emigrated to the USA and the British dominions.

Capitalism

Under the capitalist system, most people's incomes rose, while prices tended to fall. The system, however, had some serious drawbacks. Although huge amounts of wealth were produced, the great mass of people, even in the most advanced countries, were poor. They may have been a little better off than their grandparents, but they were certainly much worse off than their bosses. The gap between rich and poor was as wide as ever.

Another problem was that the system was unstable.

Left: The People's Charter of 1838 in Britain demanded votes for all adult men and other political reforms. There were violent Chartist outbreaks in several places.

Above: In the nineteenth century, most Western governments recognized the need for universal education, which they believed should no longer be a private matter, but provided by the state.

The upward movement of profits was interrupted every few years by an economic "slump." Then banks, businesses, and people went bankrupt and unemployment soared (the word "unemployment" was first used at this time). Of course, people had been unemployed before, but the spectacle of millions of

BETWEEN 1800 AND 1900 EUROPEAN POPULATION INCREASES FROM 190 TO 423 MILLION men out of work was new. It was also frightening, especially to governments which remembered the French Revolution. Serious uprisings and riots took place in most countries, although they died out after 1848, the so-called Year of Revolutions.

Economic booms and slumps were made worse because governments had no way of controlling business activities. In fact, governments believed that business should *not* be controlled. Along with "free trade" went "free enterprise" and belief in *laissez-faire*, which means leaving things alone. Governments disliked passing laws that restricted business, unless it was to stop some especially bad scandal, like the use of small children in mines. This attitude allowed fast-thinking businessmen to make huge fortunes. Some of them used methods that were dishonorable, dishonest, or even criminal.

Social Welfare

Toward the end of the nineteenth century, many laws were passed to protect ordinary people against the worst effects of the capitalist system, which had become increasingly apparent. Bismarck, the German chancellor (see pages 66–67), surprised his opponents by introducing pensions and sickness benefits for workers. Factory acts were passed in many countries to ensure decent working conditions. Unlike earlier acts of this kind, these were overseen by full-time inspectors, who made sure the laws were obeyed. In France, where a socialist joined the government for the first time in 1898, the working day was limited to ten hours. And, at last, governments recognized the need for schooling. By 1900, public schools were open in most cities in the USA, and nearly every European country had free, compulsory education.

THE POWER OF THE DOLLAR

The rapid growth of the USA was unique in history. The first transcontinental railroad was opened in 1869, and soon after, the hugely profitable steel, oil, and electrical industries began to flourish. Between 1870 and 1914, industrial growth trebled. Mining towns sprang up like mushrooms.

Agriculture also played its part. The Midwest, which produced mammoth crops of wheat, became "Europe's bread basket." Huge herds of cattle grazed pastures which had once been the sole preserve of bison, and large cities like Chicago and Cincinnati rose on the profits of the meat-packing industry. By 1900, the USA was the richest industrial nation in the world, closely followed by Germany. Britain, previously at the top of the list, was slipping down.

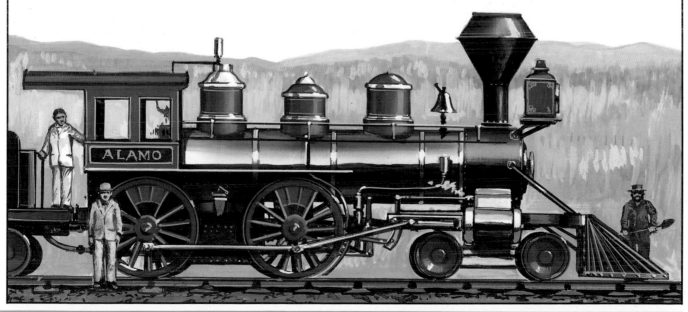

BETWEEN 1850 AND 1914 30 MILLION PEOPLE EMIGRATE FROM EUROPE TO THE USA

THE GERMAN EMPIRE

The rebellions and reform movements of the early nineteenth century were linked with a spirit of nationalism. This often took the form of a desire to be rid of foreign rule. Yet, the idea of a *nation* was quite new and was the main force behind the formation of new states in Europe.

Belgium, which had been part of the Netherlands under Napoleon, broke away in 1830 and persuaded a German prince to become its first king. At the other end of Europe, the Greeks rebelled against their Turkish Muslim rulers and, after a long struggle, gained their independence in 1829.

Nationalist revolts were not all successful. The Poles rose against their Russian rulers but, without any help from France or Britain, were crushed.

Italy

Nationalist rebellions, as the Poles discovered, needed help from the two great "liberal" powers if they were to succeed. In the nineteenth century, most of the states which together made up Italy were part of the Austrian Empire. Count Camillo Cavour, one of the leading statesmen of the day, wanted these states to be both independent and unified, and as a result of clever diplomacy gained French help against the Austrians. His cause was furthered by Giuseppe Garibaldi, a renowned soldier, who, in 1860, invaded the south with his rebel army of "Redshirts." (They were called this because of their uniforms.) Gradually, foreign rule was overthrown and the kingdom of Italy was proclaimed in 1861. Venice and Rome were added to the new nation some time later.

Prussia

Austria, like Turkey, was a failing power. Besides losing Italy, she only held on to Hungary by creating a "Dual Monarchy" in 1867, under which arrangement both countries had the same ruler, but Hungary remained a separate kingdom. In addition, Austria was losing her old authority in Germany.

The German Confederation, set up in 1815, contained 39 states. All had their own customs barriers, which prevented trade from developing. When Prussia, the strongest of the states, did away with the

GREECE BECOMES INDEPENDENT 1829 • KINGDOM OF ITALY PROCLAIMED 1861

customs barriers inside its own borders, it soon began to prosper. Gradually, other German states joined the Prussian customs union, and Prussia became the economic leader of Germany.

In 1862, Otto von Bismarck, the outstanding statesman of the age, became chief minister of Prussia. Over the next 20 years, his policies led to the creation of a German empire dominated by this state.

As a first step, Bismarck involved Austria in a war with Denmark, from which Prussia gained the province of Schleswig-Holstein. A quarrel with Austria over the result gave an excuse for the Austro-Prussian War of 1866. It lasted for just four weeks, but this was long enough to show who would be the future master of Germany.

In 1867, a North German Confederation (including some south German states) was formed, led by Prussia. As a result, France became alarmed at Prussian power, and unwisely declared war. The Franco-Prussian War (1870–1871) ended with the defeat of the French. They were forced to hand over Alsace and Lorraine, their two northern provinces, to the new German Empire, which came into existence in 1871 when Wilhelm I of Prussia was declared emperor of Germany.

The Turks

Since the seventeenth century, the power of Islam had been retreating. The Ottoman Turks lost Hungary to Austria and, more important, territories in southeast Europe to the Russians. Everywhere the Turks' Christian subjects rebelled. The Turkish state would

Far left: Giuseppe Garibaldi, the Italian nationalist guerrilla leader who, in 1860, invaded Sicily and Naples with his Thousand Redshirts in the name of a united Italy.

Left: Otto von Bismarck, the Prussian minister who was the architect of the German Empire. After he left the government in 1890, there was no one to prevent the rising tide of German nationalism from leading to European war.

have collapsed altogether had it not been supported by Britain and France, who did not want the Russians to advance any further.

Other Muslim regions were also weak. Mehemet Ali made himself master of Egypt in 1805 and adopted Western ways, but Egypt soon fell under French and British domination. Other Muslims advised a return to a stricter, purer form of Islam. Among them were the Wahhabis, who came to control much of Arabia under the protection of the princely Saud family. They were defeated in 1818, but continued to have considerable influence in the Muslim world.

KARL MARX

Karl Marx (1818–1883) was a German-born political thinker who believed that economic motives are the main force for change; he forecast a world revolution of the working class and the creation of a Communist society.

WORLD WAR I

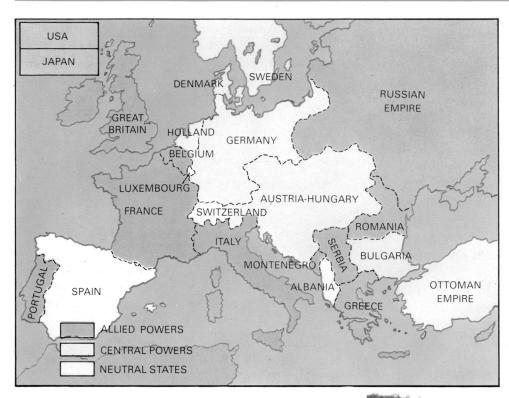

Left: World War I resulted from the division of Europe into a system of alliances, originally intended for defense, and the rising power of Germany, which upset the "balance" between rival blocks. The Allies (Britain, France, and Russia until 1917) were joined by many other states, of which the most important were Japan, Italy (joined 1915), and the USA (1917).

Europe was unusually peaceful in the late nineteenth century, but it was an ominous kind of peace. The creation of the German Empire had upset the balance of power, and the great nations of Europe hurriedly made a number of defensive alliances, which divided Europe into two hostile blocks. Germany and Austria were in one block, Britain, France, and Russia were in the other.

The Great War

A small incident, the murder of an Austrian archduke by a Serb in June 1914, was enough to start World War I. It caused Austria to threaten the Serbs, who were supported by Russia. Germany, supporting Austria, declared war on Russia. France and Britain then joined in on Russia's side. A number of other, smaller countries were also involved. Italy began as an ally of Germany but changed sides in 1915.

With little idea of what modern war was like, troops went off to fight in high spirits. Those who were not killed or crippled returned in a very different mood. The armies quickly became bogged down in defensive trenches, bombarded by artillery and machine guns. The number of casualties was horrific. Between

BRITAIN AND FRANCE DECLARE WAR AUGUST 1914 • GERMAN SURRENDER NOVEMBER 1918

August and November 1914 alone, 90,000 British, 700,000 German, and 850,000 French soldiers were killed or wounded. There were no decisive naval battles, but German submarines destroyed many merchant ships. Attacks on neutral ships brought the USA into the war in 1917. Other armies were becoming exhausted, and the arrival of fresh troops forced the Germans to surrender in 1918.

Effects of the War

About 15 million people died as a result of World War I, either in battle or from disease and starvation. The economy of Europe, especially Germany, was in ruins. The Austrian and Turkish empires were gone forever. The only "victor" was the USA, which was the strongest country in the world in 1918.

European society had changed in less obvious ways during the war. In particular, the position of women had altered. They had been forced to take over men's jobs and had shown that they could do them very well. As a result, the movement for women's rights, including the right to vote, became unstoppable.

The Russian Revolution

Failure in war and the loss of thousands of men caused rebellion in Russia in 1917. The czar (emperor) was forced to abdicate, and a republican government was set up. In six months, however, this too was overthrown by the Bolsheviks, followers of Karl Marx (see pages 66–67). The Bolsheviks were few in numbers, but they were dedicated and ruthless, and they had an inspiring leader in Lenin. They made peace with Germany and swept away the institutions of capitalist society. Russia became the Union of Soviet Socialist Republics (USSR) and local government was taken over by workers' councils, called soviets.

The Bolsheviks had expected the "workers revolution" to spread throughout Europe, but this did not happen. They had opponents at home, too, and used ruthless methods to keep themselves in power. Under Joseph Stalin, who ruled from 1924 to 1953, the Bolsheviks gained a leader who was willing to kill thousands of his compatriots to keep the Communist Party – and himself – in power.

Right: Lenin was the mastermind of the Bolshevik Revolution in Russia and became head of the new Communist government. He took Russia out of the war and nationalized land and property.

Left: The main area of fighting was Belgium and northern France, where huge battles were fought to gain or lose a few yards. These British soldiers look happy on capturing a German trench. A few months later, many of them would be lying dead in this same wasteland.

BOLSHEVIK REVOLUTION NOVEMBER 1917 • RUSSIAN CIVIL WAR 1918–1921

THE NEW DICTATORS

The Treaty of Versailles, which settled European affairs after World War I, created several new countries, including Czechoslovakia and Yugoslavia. It left the Germans feeling bitter, however.

Nationalism was the basis for creating the new states, and the war also gave Irish nationalists a chance to assert their independence of Britain. After rebellion and civil war, the Irish Free State was created in 1922. (Northern Ireland remained British.)

The Treaty of Versailles also established the League of Nations, which was intended to solve international disputes by peaceful means. However, the world was still dominated by Western countries. The Arab states, which had gained independence from the Turks, were now ruled by the French or British instead, and the newly discovered oil of the Middle East was controlled by Western businesses.

Many Europeans enjoyed a higher living standard after the war, with more time to spend on entertainments like the movies and the radio. More people were able to employ servants, and housework became easier with the invention of vacuum cleaners and electric irons. Cars and buses were becoming more common. Capitalist society, however, suffered its worst economic blow ever in 1929, when a disastrous slump put many firms out of business and caused high unemployment.

Fascism

The threat of Communist revolution and the growing industrial power of the USSR frightened other European countries. Many people responded to the threat from the extreme Left (Communism) by supporting the extreme Right in the form of Fascism.

The Fascist movement in Italy was anti-liberal and anti-democratic. Italy had suffered in World War I and, like Germany, had been disappointed by the Treaty of Versailles. Many people turned to Benito Mussolini, the tough, confident leader of the Fascists, who came to power in 1922. Although the Italian

Left: The "crash" on Wall Street (the New York Stock Exchange) in 1929 caused an economic slump.

Above: By the 1930s, radio provided home entertainment for almost everyone.

TREATY OF VERSAILLES 1919 • MUSSOLINI APPOINTED ITALIAN PRIME MINISTER 1922

Above: The economic recession of the 1930s made people angry with the existing political system. In Germany, Hitler's Nazi party, promising a glorious future for the German nation, gained power in 1933.

Right: Francisco Franco accepted help from Hitler and Mussolini to win the Spanish Civil War, but kept Spain out of World War II.

Fascists committed acts of violence and cared little for ordinary justice, they were less ruthless than some parties of the extreme Right. The Nazis were worse.

Nazi Germany

The post-war republican government in Germany was unpopular, both because it had been created by the Treaty of Versailles and because it failed to solve the severe economic problems of the early 1930s. The National Socialist (Nazi) Party, led by Adolf Hitler, played on people's bitterness. The Nazi form of nationalism was racist. According to Hitler, the Germans were a superior race and the troubles of Germany had been caused by foreigners and Jews (many Germans were Jewish). In 1933 the Nazis won power. They swept away all democratic government and established a state based on force and terror. Jews and other people considered inferior were persecuted. Millions were later murdered. Hitler also began an aggressive foreign policy, building up German military forces and taking over Austria and Czechoslovakia.

In Spain, General Francisco Franco led the Nationalists (Fascists) who gained power following civil war (1936–1939). During the war, Franco was given substantial military aid by Italy and Germany.

Communism and Fascism

The two great hostile political systems – Communism and Fascism – had much in common. Both were based on unlimited state power and the destruction of the rights of ordinary people. Democratic government survived in the USA, Britain, and France. In the USA, however, the Great Depression caused widespread misery: about 15 million people were out of work at one time. Eventually, the New Deal policies of President Franklin Roosevelt, which put a huge amount of government money into the economy and social welfare, helped the country recover.

In the Far East, Japan, a great industrial power by 1930, had an aggressive, nationalistic government, which gained control of the Chinese province of Manchuria. No strong central authority had appeared in China after the overthrow of the emperor, but Japanese aggression strengthened support not only for the ruling Kuomintang (moderate nationalist) party, which established a central government in 1928, but also for Communism.

WORLD WAR II

European domination of the world was beginning to shrink by 1939. Although the size of the European empires had actually increased slightly, Europeans ruled some countries only as caretakers for the League of Nations. The British Empire was gradually changing into the British Commonwealth of Nations, an association of independent nations which had once been British colonies.

The Coming of War

By 1938, the aggressive policies of Nazi Germany had brought Europe to the brink of war. The only large powers that could hope to check Hitler were Britain and France. In the Munich Agreement, drawn up after a conference among the British, French, Germans, and Italians in 1938, they gave permission for Germany to take over part of Czechoslovakia, where many Germans lived. Six months later Hitler – with no agreement – took over the rest of the country. He next moved against Poland, but this time Britain and France stood firm. When Hitler failed to withdraw his troops, they declared war.

Left: A British Typhoon attacks a German *panzer* (tank) column, retreating through France after the Allied invasion of Normandy. Although the success of the Normandy landings meant the Germans were bound to be defeated, they kept fighting for nearly a year.

MUNICH AGREEMENT SEPTEMBER 1938 • WAR DECLARED ON GERMANY SEPTEMBER 1939

Blitzkrieg

The Germans introduced a new type of warfare known as *Blitzkrieg*, or "lightning war", in which aircraft and fast-moving columns of tanks struck swiftly into enemy territory. Britain and France were too late to prevent the fall of Poland, and in 1940, the Germans launched new attacks. They took Norway, Denmark, Belgium, and Holland, and, finally, France. The British army on the continent scrambled back across the English Channel from Dunkirk. The Italians, sensing victory, joined in the war on Germany's side.

Britain, supported by the dominions, was the only major opponent left, but had the good fortune to be protected by the English Channel. It was supported by the Free French forces, which were based in London. The Germans could not invade until they had gained control of the air, but in the Battle of Britain, which took place between July and October 1940, they failed to defeat Britain's Royal Air Force.

In 1939, the USSR and Germany had made an agreement not to attack each other. Hitler, however, who kept his promises only as long as it suited him, ordered the invasion of the USSR in June 1941. The Germans advanced rapidly on Moscow, but then their forces became bogged down. Russian partisans resisted bravely behind German lines.

The Tide Turns

The USA was drawn into the war when the Japanese made a treacherous attack on the US fleet at Pearl Harbor, Hawaii, on December 7, 1941. The Germans and Italians declared war on the USA in support of Japan.

In 1942, the Germans were defeated at El Alamein, North Africa, by the British and, early in 1943, by the Soviets at Stalingrad. In the Pacific, the USA defeated the Japanese at Midway. In the Atlantic, German submarines, which had stopped supplies from reaching Britain from the USA, were checked.

British and US forces invaded occupied France in June 1944. A landing had also been made in Italy, where Mussolini was overthrown, and the USSR was advancing in the east. Hitler fought to the last before committing suicide as the Soviets entered Berlin in April 1945. The Japanese surrendered when the USA dropped nuclear bombs on Hiroshima and Nagasaki in August 1945.

During the war, millions of people had been killed, including about 6 million Jews, gassed in concentration camps. European civilization had received a blow from which it could only recover in a different form. Its future depended on the two great world powers, the USA and the USSR, who were already confronting each other angrily amid the wreckage.

Below: World War II was the first war in which air power was decisive. The Japanese-American war for control of the Pacific was fought largely by battleships and aircraft launched from carriers like this.

Right: The Japanese refused to surrender even when losing. To end the war, the USA dropped atomic bombs on two Japanese cities.

JAPANESE ATTACK PEARL HARBOR DECEMBER 1941 • GERMAN SURRENDER MAY 1945

THE POST-WAR WORLD

Left: After World War II, Germany was divided into Communist East and democratic West. Many people from the East tried to flee to the more prosperous West, so a great barrier was built along the border. In Berlin, the barrier took the form of a huge wall, and the Brandenburg Gate, shown here, was the main crossing point.

Right: In 1946, civil war broke out in China between the Nationalist government and the Communists, led by Mao Tse-Tung, whose portrait these marchers are carrying.

The victors of World War II founded the United Nations (UN) to maintain world peace. It has not always succeeded, but its agencies have done valuable work for world health, education and welfare.

The Cold War

In the late 1940s, the world was dominated by the two superpowers. The USSR had its "satellites" in Eastern Europe, whose Communist governments were controlled from Moscow. The USA was supported by democratic Western Europe, which recovered quickly from the war, thanks to US aid. Hostility between the two power blocs was so strong that people spoke of a "cold" war between them. The fear of nuclear weapons helped to prevent a "hot" war. In 1962, a serious world crisis followed the US discovery that Soviet nuclear weapons had been placed in Cuba. War was avoided when the USSR removed them.

Wars between Communist and democratic forces were fought in other countries. In the Korean War of 1950–1953, the UN, led by the USA, supported democratic South Korea against the Communist North, which was aided by China. In the 1960s, the Americans tried to prevent a Communist takeover of South Vietnam and became involved in a grim war, which ended in their defeat in 1973.

The superpowers also had internal problems. In the USA the biggest of these was the status of blacks, who in parts of the country were not even allowed to vote. The Civil Rights movement in the 1960s, led by activists such as Martin Luther King, ended the worst injustices. The USSR was faced with riots and rebellion against Communist domination in Eastern European nations, where living standards had fallen far behind the capitalist West.

To improve cooperation between European countries, the European Economic Community (EEC) was

UN FOUNDED 1945 • PEOPLE'S REPUBLIC OF CHINA FOUNDED 1949

Below: A North Vietnamese soldier keeps watch for US airplanes from a high lookout post in the forest. The Vietnam War resulted in the Americans' first military defeat ever.

founded in 1957, and by 1990 it consisted of 12 member states.

The Far East

In China, the Kuomintang government was defeated by the Communists under Mao Tse-tung. It withdrew to the island of Taiwan, and, in 1949, the Communist People's Republic of China was formed on the mainland. Japan, under US occupation, became a democratic state and, by the 1980s, its economic skills had made it the richest country in the world.

The Third World

World War II marked the end of European imperialism, although it took many years – and much violence – for some colonies to become independent.

In India, full independence was gained in 1947. Because Hindus and Muslims failed to agree, the country was split into India and Pakistan. (In 1971 East Pakistan broke away to become Bangladesh.) Most African colonies became independent by 1970, but there were some exceptions, and independence was sometimes followed by crippling civil wars. French settlers in Algeria fought long and fiercely to remain French, but the country became independent in 1961, while Portugal held onto Angola and Mozambique until 1974. South Africa became a white-dominated republic, practicing *apartheid*, or separation of the races, which meant keeping black Africans poor and voteless. In the 1980s some reforms took place and *apartheid* slowly disappeared.

The new state of Israel, created out of the mainly Arab country of Palestine in 1948, aroused the hostility of Arab nations. With US backing, Israel not only survived but increased its territory during a series of brief wars with its Arab neighbors.

Many South American countries were taken over by dictators. This encouraged Communism, which worried the USA, since Cuba's Communist revolution in 1950 had given the USSR a base in the Americas.

Rich and Poor

The gap between the rich and poor of the world increased. Poor countries borrowed huge sums from the rich, which they were completely unable to repay. The under-developed countries were often called the "Third World," the other two being the capitalist West and the Communist bloc.

KOREAN WAR 1950–1953 • CUBAN MISSILE CRISIS 1962 • VIETNAM WAR 1964–1973

NEW WAYS OF LIVING

In the twentieth century, amazing advances in communications, which people living only 100 years ago would never have believed possible, have made the world a much smaller place. Through radio, news can be broadcast throughout the world in minutes. Since the 1970s, television pictures have been broadcast equally fast, using satellites in space to "bounce" the signal around the earth's curve. Ordinary people can speak to anyone in the world by telephone, and fax and telex machines can send written messages and copies of documents almost anywhere instantly. Improvements in communications have also affected business, which has become international, with companies opening offices in many different countries.

Speedy methods of travel have also opened up the world. People can be transported to any part of the globe in a few hours by jet airplane. Modern roads and mass-produced cars allow people to travel long distances quickly in their own vehicles.

Of all the advances in transport and communications in the twentieth century, the most amazing has been the conquest of space. Sputnik 1, the first space satellite, was launched by the USSR in October 1957, and the first manned space flight was made in April 1961 by Yuri Gagarin, the Soviet cosmonaut. In July 1969, US astronauts, in their spacecraft Apollo 11, were the first men to land on the moon.

The Environment

Photographs of the earth taken from space have made people realize that it is a fragile and beautiful planet and that pollution and the thoughtless use of natural resources will endanger its future.

By the 1980s, scientists had discovered that several dangerous environmental changes were already beginning. One of these was called the "greenhouse effect," a term which describes the warming up of the earth's atmosphere as a result of the release of gases from power stations, cars, and so on. This warming leads in turn to the melting of ice near the poles, which raises the sea level. Such a major change in climate could cause floods, leaving some of the world's largest cities, and even some whole countries, under water.

The greenhouse effect is being accelerated by the destruction of rainforests. These are being cut down for farmland and timber at a frightening rate.

Below: In the past twenty years, the speed of travel and the number of travelers have increased enormously. Air travel became possible for most people, but the railroads also played a part, especially services like the French High-Speed Train, which runs between Paris and Lyons, and can reach a speed of 180 mph.

FIRST MANNED SPACE FLIGHT 1961 • GORBACHEV BECOMES SOVIET LEADER 1985

Right: When Mikhail Gorbachev (shown here with President Reagan) came to power in the USSR, he began reforms to give the Soviet people more choice and freedom, and to end the Cold War.

Left: The beautiful photographs of the Earth taken from spaceships and satellites helped to make people realize that it is a fragile planet and must be carefully looked after by its inhabitants.

Energy

Since the Industrial Revolution, human beings have used increasing amounts of energy from coal, oil, and gas. These fuels are gradually being used up. One twentieth-century solution to the need for supplies of energy was nuclear power. After the explosion of a nuclear plant at Chernobyl in the USSR in 1986, however, nuclear power has become less popular.

Political Changes

Since 1945, there have not been any world wars, but many lesser ones, mostly in the Third World. The Iran–Iraq War (1980–1988) was particularly harsh.

In the 1980s, the Cold War came to an end, largely through the endeavors of Mikhail Gorbachev, the man who became general secretary of the Soviet Communist Party in 1985. Under his policy of *glasnost* (openness), the USSR became a more liberal state, giving increased power to ordinary people and loosening its control over its satellite states. Communist East Germany united with democratic West Germany in October 1990. Free democratic elections were organized in countries formerly subject to state Communism, and Soviet troops in Europe were greatly reduced. When a world crisis developed as a result of Iraq's invasion of Kuwait in 1990, the USA and USSR united to condemn Iraq.

CHERNOBYL EXPLOSION IN USSR 1986 • BERLIN WALL DISMANTLED 1989

INDEX

Figures in italics refer to captions.

Aachen 20, *20*
Abbas the Great, Shah 44, *45*
Abbasid Caliphate 28, 29
Aeschylus 15
African civilizations 60–61, *60, 61*
Ajanta *37*
Akbar, Emperor 45
Alexander the Great 14, 15
Ali, Mehemet 67
alphabet, invention of 13, *13*
American Civil War 58, *59*
American War of Independence 51, *51*, 52
Amida Buddha *34*
Angkor 37
apartheid 75
Apollo 11 76
Aristotle 14–15
Armada 46, 47, *47*
Ashikaga shogunate 34, 35
Asoka 36, *36*
Assyrian empire 11, 13, 18
Athens 14, *15*
Augsburg, Diet of 43
Augustus, Emperor 17
Aurangzeb, Emperor 45
Austro-Prussian War 67
Avignon 25
Aztecs 40–41

Babylonian empire 10, 11, 18
Baghdad 20, 28, 29
Basil II, Emperor 26–7
Battle of Britain 73
Becket, Thomas 25
Beijing 33
Bell, Alexander Graham 57
Benin 60
Berlin Wall 77
Bismarck, Otto von 65, 67, *67*
Black Death 30
Blitzkrieg 73
Boer War 61
Bolívar, Simon 63, *63*
Bolshevik Revolution 69, *69*
Bolsheviks 69
Borodino, Battle of 53
Boston Tea Party 51
British Empire 62, 72
Buddha 36
Buddhism 33, 34, 36, *36*, 37
Byzantium 17, 20, 26–7, *26, 27*

Caesar, Julius 17, *17*

Calvin, John 43, *43*
Cambodia 37
canals 56
Cape Town 61
capitalism 39, 45, 47, 64, 65, 70
cars 57, *57*, 70, 76
Carthage 13
Cartwright, Edmund 55
Catherine of Aragon 43
Catherine the Great 48
Cavaliers *49*
cave paintings 7
Cavour, Count Camillo 66
Charlemagne 20, *20*, 24
Charles I, King 49
Charles V, Emperor 42, 43, *44*
Chaucer, Geoffrey 31
Chernobyl 77
China, foundation of Republic of 74, 75
Chinese civilization 32–3, *32*
Cholas 37
Christian Church 24–5, *25*, 38, 42
Christianity 16–19, *19*, 21, 26, 29, *29*, 44, 45
Civil Rights movement 74
Classical period 14, 15
Clovis 20
Code Napoléon 53
Cody, "Buffalo Bill" 59
Cold War 74–5, 77, *77*
Coligny, Admiral *47*
Colosseum, Rome *17*
Columbus, Christopher 40, *40, 41*
Commonwealth 72
communications 57, 76
Communism 69, 70, 74, *74*, 75, 77
Confucianism 36
Confucius 32
Constantinople 17, 20, 21, 26, 27, 29, 44, 45
Cook, Captain James 62
Copernicus, Nicolaus 39
Cordoba *29*
Cortés, Hernán 41
Counter-Reformation 46
Crete 12, *12*
Cromwell, Oliver 49, *49*
Crusades 28, 29
Cuban Missile Crisis 74, 75
cuneiform writing 10
Cyrus the Great 11

Damascus 28
David, King 18
Delhi 45
Delhi Sultanate 37
Diaspora 18
Dorians 13
Drake, Sir Francis 46
Dunkirk 73

East India Company 45
Egypt 8–9, *8, 9*, 12, 18, 28
El Alamein 73
Emancipation Proclamation (1863) 58, 59
English Civil War 49
Erasmus 38
Euphrates River 10, *10*
Euripides 15
European Economic Community (EEC) 74–5
Evans, Sir Arthur 12

Fascism 70–71
feudalism 22–3, 30
Ford, Henry 57
Franco-Prussian War 67
Franco, General Francisco 71, *71*
Franks 20
French Revolution 52–3, 65

Gagarin, Yuri 76
Gama, Vasco da 41, *41*
Ganges River 37, *37*
Garibaldi, Giuseppe 66, *67*
Genghis Khan 33
German Confederation 66–7
Germany *74*
Ghana 60
Giza 8, *9*
glasnost 77
Gorbachev, Mikhail 76, 77, *77*
Granada 29
Great Depression 71
Great Northern War 48
Great Pyramid of King Khufu, Giza 8
Greco, El 26
Greece 12–15, *14, 15*, 38
greenhouse effect 76
Gregory VII, Pope 25
Guise, Duke of 46
Gupta empire 36, 37
Gustavus Adolphus, King of Sweden 47
Gutenberg, Johannes *39*

Hadrian, Emperor 17
Hagia Sophia *27*
Han dynasty 32, 33
Hanging Gardens of Babylon *10*
Hapsburg dynasty 39, 47
Harappa 11
Hargreaves, James 54, 55
Hastings, Battle of 22
Hebrews 18, 19
Hellenistic age 15
Henry II, King 25
Henry IV, Emperor 24, 25
Henry VIII, King 43
Henry of Navarre 46, *47*
Heraclius, Emperor 26
Hinduism 36
Hiroshima 73
Hitler, Adolf 71, *71*, 72, *73*
Holy Roman Empire 47
Homer 13
Horace 17
Hudson Bay Company 51
Huguenots 46
Hundred Years' War 30, 31
Hungary 44

Iceland 21
Incas 41, *41*
India 11, 36–7, *36, 37*, 44, 45
Indus River valley 11, *11*
Industrial Revolution 54–5, 56, 77
Innocent III, Pope 24, 25
Inquisition 25
Iran–Iraq War 77
Iraq 28, 29
Isfahan 44
Islam 18, 20, 26, 28–9, *29*, 44, 60
Israelites 18
Italy 22, 26, 38

James II, King 49
Japanese civilization 34–5, *34, 35*
Jenne mosque *61*
Jericho 6
Jerusalem 18, *28*, 29
Jesuits 46
Jesus of Nazareth 18, 19, *19*
Jews 18, 19, 71, 73
Judaism 18, 19
Judea 18
Justinian I, Emperor 26, *26, 27*

Kamakura Period 34

King, Martin Luther 74
Knossos 12
Korea 32
Korean War 74, 75
Kubilai Khan 32, 33
Kuwait, invasion of 77
Kyoto Period 34

laissez-faire 65
League of Nations 70, 72
Lenin 69, 69
Leonardo da Vinci 38–9, 39
Lepanto, Battle of 45
Lincoln, Abraham 58, 59, 59
Livy 17
Louis XIV, King 48, 48, 49
Louis XVI, King 52, 53
Luther, Martin 42, 43, 43

Machu Picchu 41
Magellan, Ferdinand 40, 41, 41
Mahrattas 45
Malaya 77
Manchu dynasty 33
Mao Tse-Tung 74, 75
Marie Antoinette 52, 53
Marx, Karl 67, 69
Massachusetts 50
Maurya empire 36
Mecca 28
Medieval Europe 30–31, 30
Medina 28
Menes, King 8
Mesopotamia 10, 10
Mexican War 63
Michelangelo 38, 39
Middle Ages 21, 31, 31
Minamoto shogunate 34
Minamoto Yoritomo 34
Ming dynasty 32, 33
Minoans 12, 12
Minos, King 12
Mogul empire 37, 44, 45
Mohenjo-daro 11
monasteries 24, 25
Mongols 32, 32, 33,
    34, 37, 45
Monroe Doctrine 63
Morocco, Sultan of 60
Morse, Samuel 57
Moses 18, 19
Muhammad 28, 28, 29
mummies 9
Munich Agreement 72
Murasaki Shikibu 34
Mussolini, Benito 70, 71
Mycenae 12–13, 14

Nadir Shah, King of Persia 45
Nagasaki 73
Nanking 32
Nantes, Edict of 46
Napoleon Bonaparte 53, 53
nationalism 39, 70
Nazism 71, 71, 72
Nero, Emperor 17
New Babylon 10
New Deal 71
newspaper industry 57
Nile River 8, 9, 11
95 Theses 42, 43
Nō drama 34
Norman Age 22–3
Normandy 21
Normandy landings 72

Opium War 62, 63
Otto the Great 24
Ottoman empire 44–5
Ovid 17
Oxford University 23

Panama Canal 57
Papacy 24, 25, 26, 42
Paris, University of 23
Parthenon, Athens 15, 15
Pearl Harbor 73
Peasants' Revolt (1381) 30
Peasants' Revolt (1524) 42, 43
People's Charter (1838) 64
Persia 11, 15, 26, 28, 29, 44,
    44, 45, 45
Peter the Great 48
pharaohs 8, 8
Philip, King of Macedon 15
Philip II, King 46, 47
Philippines 63
Philistines 18
Phoenicians 13, 13
Pizarro, Francisco 41
plow, invention of 7
Poland, and Russia 48
Polo, Marco 32
postal system 57
pottery 7, 7, 32, 33
printing 38, 39
Protestantism 43, 43
pyramids 8, 9

radio 70
railroads 56, 57, 57, 76
Rashid, Harun ar- 29
Reagan, Ronald 77
Redshirts 66, 67
Reformation 39, 42–3, 46
Reims Cathedral 31

Renaissance 38–9, 39, 40
Richard I, King 29
roads 57, 76
Roman Empire 16–17, 16, 19,
    19, 20, 26
Rome 13, 16, 17, 17, 18, 20,
    25, 26, 38
Romulus Augustus,
    Emperor 17
Roosevelt, Franklin 71
Roundheads 49
Rousseau, Jean-Jacques 52
Russian Civil War 69
Russian Revolution 69

Safavid dynasty 44
St. Bartholomew's Day
    Massacre 46, 47
Saladin 29
Santa Maria 40
satellite 76, 77
Scandinavians 21
serfs 23, 30
Seven Wonders of the
    World 10
Seven Years' War 50, 51
Shah Jahan, Emperor 45
Shintoism 34
ships 57
silk 32, 32, 33
Sino-Japanese War 62, 63
Sistine Chapel 38
slavery 58, 61
Solomon, Temple of 18
Sophocles 15
space flight 76
Spanish Civil War 71, 71
Spanish Succession 49
Sphinx 9
Sputnik 1 76
Sri Lanka 37
Stalin, Joseph 69
Stone Age 6
Suez Canal 57
Suleiman the Magnificent
    44, 45
Sumerian civilization 10, 11
Sung dynasty 32, 33
Sweden 47, 48
Syria 28

Tacitus 17
Taiping Rebellion 62, 63
Taj Mahal 45, 45
Tamils 37
T'ang dynasty 32, 33
tea drinking ceremony 34
telephones 57, 76

television 76
Ten Commandments 19
Tenochtitlán 40, 40, 41
Thirty Years' War 47
Thor 20
Tibet 32
Tigris River 10, 10
Timurlane 37
Tokugawa shogunate 35
tombs, Egyptian 9
trades unions 55, 55
Trafalgar, Battle of 53
Trevithick, Richard 56
Troy 13
Tull, Jethro 54, 54
Turkey 26, 27, 29, 45, 67

Umayyad Caliphate 28
unemployment 64–5, 70
United Nations 74
Ur 10, 11

Valois 39
Venice 30, 38
Verdun, Treaty of 20
Vereeniging, Treaty of 61
Versailles 48, 48
Versailles, Treaty of 70
Vesalius, Andreas 39
Vienna 45
Vietnam War 75, 75
Vikings 21, 21
Virgil 17
Voltaire 52

Wall Street Crash 70
Washington, George 51, 51
Waterloo, Battle of 53
Watt, James 54, 55
Westphalia, Peace of 47
wheel, invention of 7
Wilhelm I of Prussia 67
William of Orange 49
William the Silent 46
Winter Palace, St Petersburg
    48
World War I 68–9, 68, 69
World War II 71, 72–3,
    72, 73
Worms, Diet of 42

Yellow River 32
Yuan dynasty 33

Zen Buddhism 34
Zimbabwe 60, 60
Zulu War 61
Zwingli, Huldrych 43

ACKNOWLEDGMENTS

The publishers would like to thank the following organizations and individuals for their kind permission to reproduce the pictures in this book:

Associated Press 71; The Bridgeman Art Library, London 9 bottom, 32, 45 top, 56–7, /Private Collection 49; The British Museum, London/ Bridgeman Art Library, London 25; Deutsch Fotothek, Dresden 67 top; Mary Evans Picture Library 38–9, 43, 46–7, 59 top, 62, 64, 66 left, 69 right, 70; Werner Forman Archive 21 bottom, 27 left, 29, 34, 63 top; Giraudon/Bridgeman Art Library, London 52; Barbara Heller/Robert Aberman 60; Michael Holford 6 top, 11, 13, 17, 21 top, 28, 33, 41; The Hutchison Library 45 bottom, 61, 63 bottom, 75 bottom, /Robert Francis 9 top, /Patricio Goycolea 36–7, /Jenny Pate 6 bottom; By courtesy of the Imperial War Museum, London 68–9; NASA 76; Rex Features/Sipa 75 top, 77; Trades Union Congress 55; Vatican Museums and Galleries, Rome/Bridgeman Art Library, London 38 left; By Courtesy of the Board of Trustees of the V&A, London/Bridgeman Art Library, London 27 right; Windsor Castle, Royal Library. © 1990 Her Majesty The Queen 39 right; Zefa Picture Library 20, 48, 73

Illustrations by:

Arthur Barbosa (Virgil Pomfret Agency) – pages 48, 49, 66
George Fryer (Bernard Thornton Artists) – pages 8, 27, 42–43, 52, 64, 71
Tony Gibbons (Bernard Thornton Artists) – pages 72 and 73
Terry Hadler (Bernard Thornton Artists) – 40 left, 65, 71
Graham Humphreys (Virgil Pomfret Agency) – pages 58–59
Roy Hutchins (Linden Artists) – pages 56 and 57
Bill Le Fever – page 70
Sue Mackenzie – page 53
The Maltings Partnership – pages 10–11, 11, 18–19, 22, 23, 24–25, 46–47, 54, 55, 76–77
Rob McCaig – pages 16–17, 17, 50, 51
Robert Price – pages 7, 12, 13, 14, 15 top, 20–21, 30, 31
Tony Smith (Virgil Pomfret Agency) – pages 36, 36–37, 40–41
Ann Winterbotham – pages 29, 34, 35, 44, 61
Gerald Wood – pages 19 and 32

All illustrations in top right-hand corners by Bill Le Fever, except: page 7 (Robert Price), pages 11 and 77 (The Maltings Partnership), pages 27, 43 and 71 (George Fryer, Bernard Thornton Artists), pages 29 and 61 (Ann Winterbotham), page 57 (Roy Hutchins, Linden Artists), page 67 (Arthur Barbosa, Virgil Pomfret Agency), page 73 (Tony Gibbons, Bernard Thornton Artists)

Maps on pages 8, 10, 16, 20, 26, 28, 41, 44, 60, 68 by Peter Bull Art Studios

The illustrations in the top right-hand corners of the right-hand pages in this book show the following:

Page 7, Early molded pot; page 9, Death mask of Tutankhamen; page 11, Indus River valley seal; page 13, 'Mask of Agamemnon' from Mycenae; page 15, Coin from the reign of Alexander the Great; page 17, the Pont du Gard, France, a Roman aqueduct; page 19, Torah scroll containing the five books of Moses; page 21, Charlemagne; page 23, Detail from the Bayeux Tapestry (c.1080) depicting the Battle of Hastings; page 25, Pope Innocent III; page 27, Justinian; page 29, Bedouin Arab; page 31, stained glass window; page 33, Ming dynasty shoulder jar; page 35, the Amida Buddha; page 37, gold figure of the Hindu god Siva; page 39, the Cathedral, Florence; page 41, Aztec mask; page 43, Martin Luther; page 45, the Taj Mahal; page 47, cannon from the English warship Mary Rose; page 49, the emblem of Louis XIV, the Sun King; page 51, the US flag, 1776; page 53, Bonnet of a Jacobin revolutionary; page 55, Jethro Tull's seed drill; page 57, Early telephone; page 59, the Statue of Liberty, New York; page 61, Camel train across the Sahara Desert; page 63, African wood carving of a European missionary; page 65, Victorian schoolbooks and slate; page 67, Bismarck; page 69, British Vickers machine gun from World War I; page 71, Nazi swastika emblem; page 73, the aircraft carrier USS Hornet; page 75, the Brandenburg gate, Berlin; page 77, French High-Speed Train

Illustrations in the pull out time chart show, from left to right:

Woman kneading dough; 'Mask of Agamemnon' from Mycenae; South American ceramic figures and decorated plate; Japanese samurai; the Spanish Armada; Aztec warrior; the Mogul emperor Shah Jahan, with an attendant; the emblem of Napoleon; Bag of Californian gold; Wagon train traveling to the West; Mahatma Gandhi; British Spitfire aeroplane and the Nazi emblem; President John F. Kennedy

TIME CHART

ASIA AND AFRICA

B.C.
- **c.9000** Beginning of settled farming
- **c.4000** First use of metal
- **c.3100** Egypt united under King Menes
- **c.3000** First Sumerian cities
- **c.2600** Rise of Indus River valley civilization
- **c.2100** Rise of Babylon
- **c.1200** Hebrew exodus from Egypt
- **c.720** Assyria at height of power
- **321** Maurya empire in India
- **206** Han dynasty in China

A.D.
- **29** Crucifixion of Jesus
- **146** Rome destroys Carthage
- **320** Gupta empire in northern India
- **552** Buddhism reaches Japan
- **618** T'ang dynasty in China
- **638** Arabs conquer Jerusalem
- **960** Sung dynasty in China
- **c.1000** Building at Zimbabwe in Southeast Africa
- **1099** First Crusade captures Jerusalem
- **1187** Saladin takes Jerusalem
- **1279** Yuan (Mongol) dynasty in China
- **c.1300** Rise of Ottoman Turks

EUROPE

B.C.
- **c.6500** Beginning of settled farming
- **c.2500** Minoan civilization in Crete
- **c.2000** First Phoenician cities
- **c.1600** Mycenaean civilization in Greece
- **c.800** Rise of Greek city-states
- **509** Roman republic founded
- **338** Macedonians conquer Greece

A.D.
- **43** Romans invade Britain
- **330** Constantinople founded
- **370** Huns invade Europe
- **395** Roman Empire divided in two
- **410** Visigoths sack Rome
- **486** Frankish kingdom founded
- **711** Muslims invade Spain
- **793** First Viking raids
- **800** Charlemagne crowned in Rome
- **911** Normandy granted to Vikings
- **1066** Normans conquer England
- **1071** Seljuk Turks defeat Byzantines at Battle of Manzikert
- **c.1150** First European universities founded
- **1204** Fourth Crusade captures Constantinople

AMERICAS AND OTHER REGIONS

A.D.
- **c.300** Rise of Mayan cities in Central America
- **c.1100** Toltecs build their capital at Tula in Mexico
- **c.1150** Decline of Toltecs

ASIA AND AFRICA

1338 Ashikaga shogunate in Japan
1341 Black Death begins in Asia
1368 Ming dynasty in China
1398 Timurlane invades India and destroys Delhi
1421 Peking becomes capital of China
1526 Mogul dynasty in India
1546 Mali captured by Songhai
1591 Destruction of Songhai empire

EUROPE

1305 Popes move to Avignon in France
1337 Hundred Years' War between France and England (ends 1453)
1348 Black Death arrives in Europe
1378 Great Schism (rival popes in Rome and Avignon)
1381 Peasants' Revolt in England
1453 Ottoman Turks capture Constantinople
1453 First book printed using moveable type
1492 Arab kingdom of Granada conquered by Christian forces
1517 Martin Luther attacks Church practices
1541 John Calvin founds his church in Geneva
1545 Council of Trent; Counter-Reformation begins
1568 Revolt of the Netherlands against Spain
1571 Ottomans defeated at Battle of Lepanto
1588 Spanish Armada sent against English

AMERICAS AND OTHER REGIONS

1325 Aztecs found their capital at Tenochtitlán
c.1450 Incan empire established
1492 Columbus discovers New World
1493 First Spanish colony established in New World
1493 Treaty of Tordesillas divides New World between Spain and Portugal
1497 John Cabot discovers North America
1521 Hernán Cortés conquers Aztecs
1522 One of Ferdinand Magellan's ships completes first around-the-world voyage
1534 Francisco Pizarro conquers Incas
1534 Jacques Cartier explores Canada

ASIA AND AFRICA

1603 Tokugawa shogunate in Japan
1644 Manchu (Ch'ing) dynasty in China
1652 Cape Colony founded
1707 Death of Aurangzeb, last major Mogul emperor
1757 British defeat French at Battle of Plassey
1798 Napoleon invades Egypt
1805 Mehemet Ali gains control in Egypt
1830 French conquest of Algeria begins
1835 Great Trek of Boers from Cape Colony
1839 Opium War between British and Chinese (ends 1842)
1842 Britain acquires Hong Kong on lease
1850 Taiping Rebellion in China (ends 1864)
1869 Suez Canal opened
1879 Zulu War
1882 British occupy Egypt
1894 Sino-Japanese War (ends 1895)
1899 Boer War (ends 1902)
1900 Boxer Rebellion in China

EUROPE

1609 Dutch gain independence from Spain
1618 Thirty Years' War begins (ends 1648)
1642 English Civil War begins (ends 1645)
1652 Anglo-Dutch Wars begin (end 1674)
1683 Turks besiege Vienna
1688 Glorious Revolution in England; William of Orange becomes king
1702 War of Spanish Succession begins (ends 1713)
1709 Russians defeat Swedes at Battle of Poltava
1740 War of Austrian Succession begins (ends 1748)
1756 Seven Years' War begins (ends 1763)
1789 French Revolution begins
1804 Napoleon makes himself Emperor of France
1812 Napoleon's Russian expedition
1815 Napoleon defeated at Waterloo
1848 Year of Revolutions
1861 Kingdom of Italy established
1870 Franco-Prussian War begins (ends 1871)
1871 German Empire proclaimed

AMERICAS AND OTHER REGIONS

1607 First English colony in North America
1608 French colony of Quebec founded
1620 Pilgrim Fathers arrive in America
1759 British capture Quebec from French
1775 American War of Independence begins (ends 1783)
1776 American Declaration of Independence signed
1788 First British colony in Australia
1789 George Washington becomes first US President
1803 Louisiana Purchase opens West to American settlers
1810 Independence wars begin in South America
1846 Mexican War begins (ends 1848)
1861 American Civil War begins (ends 1865)
1865 US President Abraham Lincoln assassinated
1867 Canada becomes a dominion of the British Empire
1867 USA purchases Alaska from Russia
1898 Spanish-American War

ASIA AND AFRICA

1910 Union of South Africa established as a British dominion
1911 China becomes a republic
1922 Egypt gains independence from Britain
1929 Gandhi begins campaign of civil disobedience in India
1936 Italy annexes Ethiopia
1937 Japan invades China
1947 India and Pakistan gain independence from Britain
1948 State of Israel founded
1949 People's Republic of China founded
1950 Korean War begins (ends 1953)
1956 Britain and France invade Suez Canal Zone in Egypt
1964 Beginning of US involvement in Vietnam War (ends 1973)
1971 East Pakistan becomes independent Bangladesh
1979 USSR invades Afghanistan (withdraws 1989)
1979 Islamic Republic proclaimed in Iran
1980 Rhodesia becomes independent
1980 Iran–Iraq War begins (ends 1988)
1990 Iraq invades Kuwait

EUROPE

1905 Rebellion in Russia
1914 World War I begins (ends 1918)
1917 Russian Revolution
1919 Treaty of Versailles
1920 League of Nations founded
1922 Irish Free State established
1922 Benito Mussolini gains power in Italy
1933 Adolf Hitler gains power in Germany
1936 Spanish Civil War begins (ends 1939)
1939 World War II begins (ends 1945)
1945 United Nations founded
1956 USSR crushes revolt in Hungary
1957 European Economic Community founded
1961 Berlin Wall built
1968 USSR crushes reform in Czechoslovakia
1969 British troops sent to Northern Ireland
1985 Mikhail Gorbachev becomes general secretary of the Soviet Communist Party
1989 Anti-Communist revolutions in Eastern Europe
1990 East and West Germany re-united

AMERICAS AND OTHER REGIONS

1911 Revolution in Mexico
1914 Panama Canal opened
1917 USA enters World War I
1929 Wall Street Crash starts Great Depression worldwide
1933 US President Franklin Roosevelt introduces New Deal program
1941 USA enters World War II
1943 Juan Perón gains power in Argentina
1959 Fidel Castro leads revolution in Cuba
1962 Cuban Missile Crisis
1963 US President J. F. Kennedy assassinated
1974 US President Richard Nixon resigns after Watergate scandal
1982 Falklands War between Argentina and Britain